Table Of Contents

Bulletin Boards ....

Welcome students on the first day of school with this poppin' good bulletin board. Label popcorn cutouts with student names to post on the board. Use the patterns on page 21 to make this display.

Becky Shanklin
Corinth, MS

Use the pattern on page 22 to create this "cat-chy" bulletin board. After a discussion of school rules, have students list ways to maintain harmony within the class on note cutouts. Post on a bulletin board as a reminder that rule breakers create a sour note for everyone else.

Sharon Wright
Overland Park, KS

Post this handy board to remind your class that classroom rules count! Use the pattern on page 22 to put the finger on rules to follow during the school year.

Debbie Wiggins
Myrtle Beach, SC

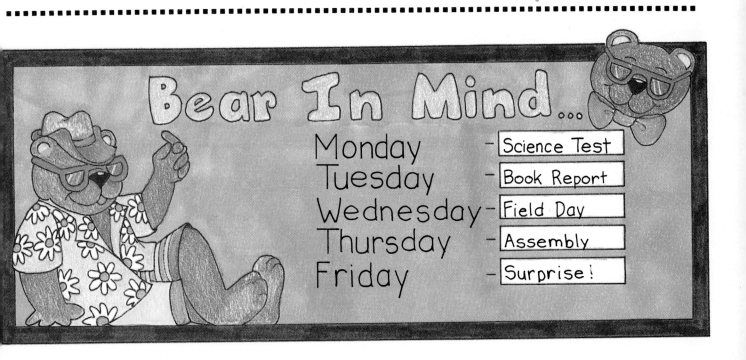

Take the "bear" out of remembering class assignments. Use the pattern on page 23 to create your furry friend. Post him by the door so students will be sure to spot special events and activities.

Jeanne Mullineaux
Geigertown, PA

Use these two eye-catching displays to involve your students in bulletin board construction—fun for the students and a welcome break for the teacher! Simply put up the headline and let your students write in their answers.

Chip Walley
Pascagoula, MS

Change this mock movie marquee frequently to motivate all kinds of good work.

Put that narrow bulletin board above your chalkboard to work as a perpetual calendar. Change month labels and event arrows for each upcoming month. Include class and school happenings, holidays, and interesting events.

Linda Bates
Garland, TX

Here is a bulletin board idea I use to stimulate reading interest. The parachutes are cut from white tagboard and string is attached to them. Then the string is wrapped around a small book.

Arnetra Townes
Norlina, NC

Give children a chance to speak their minds! Make the student cheerleaders using the pattern on page 23. Post questions that can be changed periodically, and let students write responses on sentence strips. Parents will enjoy reading the ideas when they make classroom visits.

Marjorie Edelson
Oakhurst, NJ

Show everyone at school that you are proud of your students' work. Each week display an outstanding student paper on this permanent display of smiling faces.

Debbie Wiggins
Myrtle Beach, SC

Here's an all-purpose bulletin board that's sure to be a classroom favorite. Cover the board with black background paper. Have children create robots around 9" x 12" sheets of colored construction paper. Display students' good work on the robots throughout the year.

Michelle Martin
Macon, GA

September...

Set a bulletin board aside that can be kept up for three months! Using the same background, change cutouts as the months change. Students can make colorful paper leaves for September.

Lois Elfvin
Ringoes, NJ

October...

In October, add jack-o'-lanterns and black cats.

November...

Replace jack-o'-lanterns with turkeys for November.

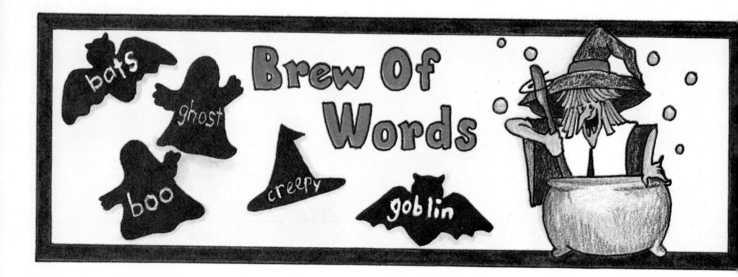

Older students will enjoy this spooky word board! Give each pupil a black construction paper shape, a Q-tip, and a small amount of liquid bleach in a glass container. The students write Halloween words with the bleach, which turns the paper white. Follow up with some creative ghost story—writing using the words on the board. See the pattern for the witch on page 24.

Karen Adams Stone
Goodland, KS

Motivate children to read by giving each a cut-out pumpkin labeled with his name. When a student reads and reports on one book (orally or written), he moves his pumpkin to the vine. For each additional book read, the student adds a facial feature—eyes, nose, mouth, teeth. Problem readers can listen to tape-recorded stories and follow along with the book.

Cindy Bolden
Tuppers Plains, OH

Halloween is the perfect time to spin a spooky story. Staple yarn into a spider-web design to hold favorite tales or poems created by your students.

Carolyn Wojtera
West Monroe, LA

Treat your students to an all-purpose Halloween bulletin board. Staple large, plastic trick-or-treat bags on the board and fill with worksheets, activity cards, etc. Students earn a treat or sticker for each activity they successfully complete.

Nancy Woodward
Richboro, PA

Try this technique for making a bright and shiny harvest wreath. Have your students draw individual fruits and vegetables. Outline each drawing with white glue and let dry overnight. Have students color inside the glue boundary, pressing down to make a solid, waxy surface. Shine each object with a tissue and cut it out. Arrange fruits and vegetables into a harvest wreath on the **bulletin board**.

Phyllis Davis
Lexington, KY

Put dad's old ties to good use! Attach to a cardboard turkey (see pattern on page 25) for the most colorful tail feathers you'll see this season.

Phyllis Roland
Henryville, IN

12

Use old holiday greeting cards to create a decorative bulletin board collage. Add a paper ribbon to stapled, overlapping cards for an easy holiday gift display.

Perry Stio
Piscataway, NJ

Celebrate the Yuletide season with great grades! Arrange noteworthy papers from all of your students into a wreath shape. Pin up with berries and a festive bow.

Rebecca L. Gibson
Camp Hill, AL

Make these 3-D candles from old magazines—big ones with more than 100 pages. Fold each page to the center and crease. Spray paint the candles or leave them unpainted, and tack to the board. Make flames from gold gift wrap or yellow paper. Use construction paper pine boughs or boughs from an artificial tree.

Sylvia McFeaters
Slippery Rock, PA

This board will encourage class unity and a cooperative spirit! Have each child decorate a construction paper house and label it with his family name beside the door. Then arrange houses on a dark background. Add spray snow for a special effect.

Barbara Hosek
Canoga Park, CA

Here's an eye-catching display with a Christmas tree theme. Students tear brightly colored pieces from magazines. Then have each student glue his pieces onto a Christmas tree cutout. Mount these collages on construction paper. Arrange them to make a striking design for a bulletin board, classroom door, or hallway.

Geraldine Fulton
Sedgewickville, MO

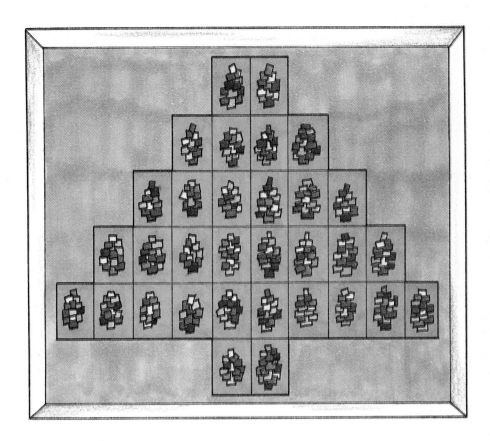

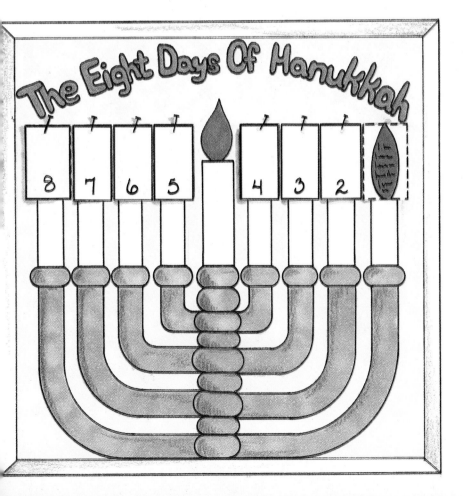

For each day of Hanukkah, remove one door to light a candle bright with fun. See the menorah pattern on page 25.

Activity under each flap:

1. Make a dreidel and label it with its four **Hebrew** letters.
2. Do a skit on the origin of Hanukkah.
3. Dip your own Hanukkah candles.
4. Make up a word game using as many Hanukkah words as you can locate.
5. Learn to do the *hora*, a traditional Hebrew dance.
6. Make some Hanukkah cards for your classmates.
7. Make some potato latkes.
8. Visit your local synagogue to learn more about Hanukkah.

This student-made New Year's display is also an opportunity for creative writing and artistry. Have students make a globe. Using tissue paper squares, students encircle the globe with a fluffy wreath. Other students decorate "children of the world" cutouts (see pattern on page 26) with fabric scraps. Add large, cut-out planets and glittered stars, rockets, and spaceships. On circular paper, students write paragraphs entitled "My Resolution For Peace in 19__" and attach them to planet cutouts.

On that first day back from Christmas vacation, have students help to decorate your January bulletin board. Give each student a strip of paper. Have him write one of his New Year's resolutions and decorate the strip. No signatures! Mount the strips around the edges of the bulletin board for a colorful border. Students have fun guessing which resolution belongs to whom. The teacher writes one too! The display is a good reminder of goals for the year.

Debbie Wiggins
Myrtle Beach, SC

Student work glistens and sparkles through this bulletin board blizzard! Write the title words on gray paper clouds and attach them to a blue background. For a 3-D effect, pin the clouds slightly away from the bulletin board. Let students add cut-out snowflakes sprinkled with glitter.

Debra J. Jezek
Hooper Bay, AK

Loving hearts combine a health unit on tobacco and alcohol with a valentine theme. To conclude that health unit, each student writes reasons he won't smoke or drink on a small, white heart and decorates it. Add hearts to large, red hearts for a huge hallway display.

Debbie Wiggins
Myrtle Beach, SC

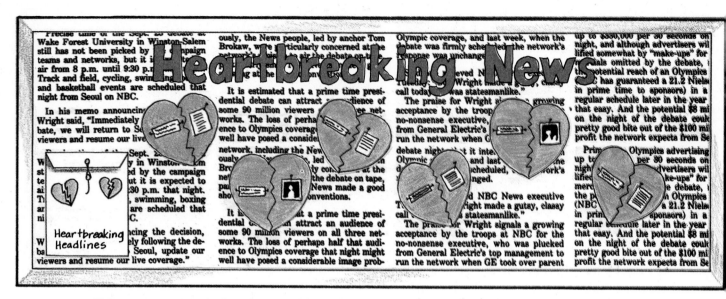

This current events bulletin board will have students looking for heartbreaking headlines. Mount red construction paper broken hearts on a newspaper background. Place a news article or picture on one piece of each broken heart. Store headlines and captions in an envelope on the board. After reading each article or studying the picture, students find the correct headline or caption and place it on the matching broken heart piece. Ask children to bring in news stories for the board, and change articles often.

Enlarge the pattern on page 26 with an overhead projector and place it on the bulletin board. Around it staple heart halves labeled with math problems. Students are to take missing halves from the storage pocket and match them up correctly. Variations: contractions, vowel sounds, vocabulary.

Sylvia McFeaters
Slippery Rock, PA

Student-made leaves and blossoms combine for the lovely effect of this working bulletin board. Have students design, make, and staple construction paper pots, leaves, and blossoms as shown. Add stems with a green marker and plant hangers made from lengths of yarn or cord. Label as shown. Students use the words to compose sentences.

Sr. Kathleen Marie
Bronx, NY

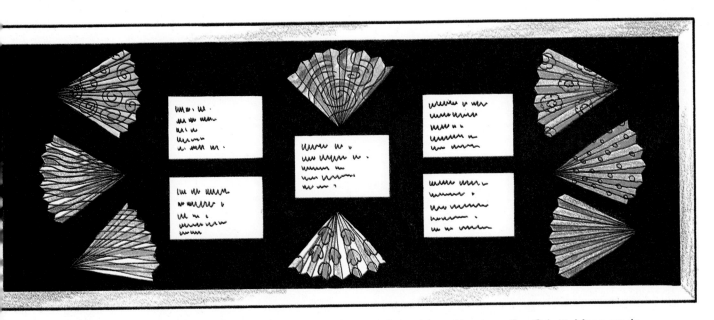

A dramatic and colorful bulletin board for springtime can be achieved by mounting Oriental fans made from wallpaper samples on a black background. Have students write haiku poems on white paper rectangles with black marker. Add a border of pleated fans. Vinyl or reflective wallpaper lends itself to this Oriental look.

Susan French
Lakeville, MA

Creating this summer bouquet will be a class project that your students are sure to enjoy. Make a master of each pattern on page 27. Duplicate both patterns on colored construction paper. (See diagram on page 27.) Students fold as indicated and cut on the dotted lines. Then, using 1/2" construction paper strips, students weave the centers. Arrange the woven flowers and butterflies on a bulletin board. Add construction paper stems and leaves to complete the board.

Carolyn Hassell
Gainesville, TX

Hallway – do in May to count down till summer

Sneakers carry students to this finish line. Have each child trace his or her shoe on white paper and cut out the shape. Have students examine the unusual patterns on the bottoms of their sneakers and color these designs on their cutouts. Mount the sneaker patterns on the bulletin board in a path to the last day of school. Number the sneakers. As each day goes by, remove a sneaker to take another step toward summer vacation.

Enlarge these patterns
to use with the
bulletin board
on page 4.

Bulletin Board Patterns

Enlarge and use with "Let's Create Harmony" on page 4.

Enlarge and use with "Remember" on page 5.

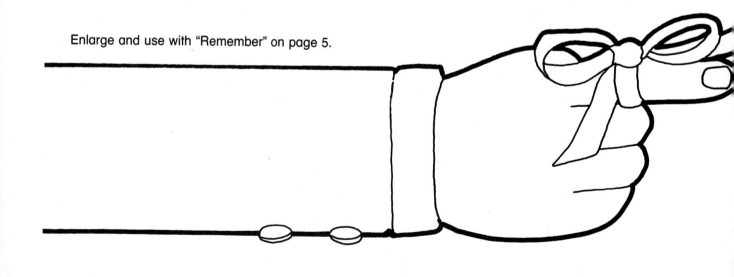

Enlarge and use with "Bear In Mind" on page 5.

Enlarge and use with "Fourth Graders Speak Up" on page 7.

Bulletin Board Pattern

Enlarge and use
with "Brew Of Words"
on page 10.

Enlarge and use with "Turkey Time" on page 12.

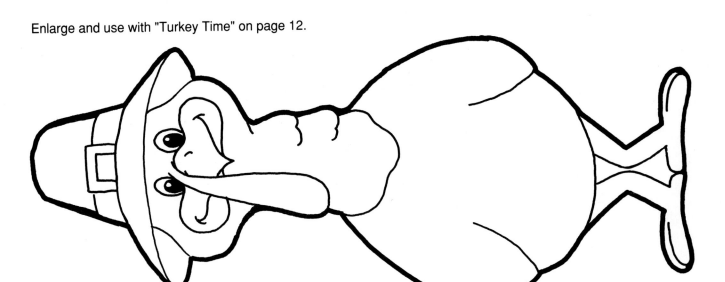

Enlarge and use with "The Eight Days of Hanukkah" on page 15.

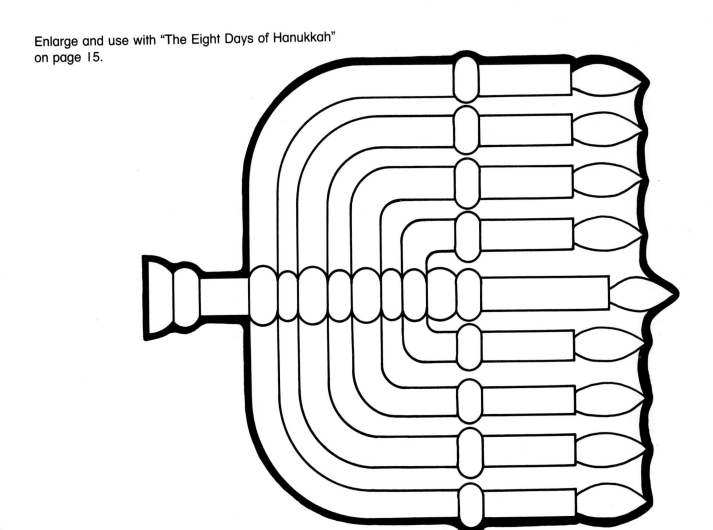

Bulletin Board Patterns

Duplicate and use with "Resolution For The New Year" on page 16.

Enlarge and use with
"Half A Heart" on page 18.

Bulletin Board Patterns

Duplicate on construction paper
to use with "Summer Garden"
on page 20.

Fold line—
Fold here;
then cut.

↑ FOLD LINE ↑

↑ FOLD LINE ↑

File Folder Ideas

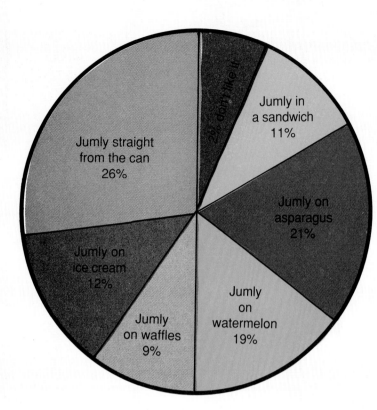

How Do You Eat Your Jumly?

A spoonful of Jumly makes this circle graph a tasty trea Cut out the worksheet and graph, and glue them inside a folder. (You may wish to duplicate page 27 before doing t step.) Write the answer key on the back of the folder.

Sylvia McFeaters
Slippery Rock, PA
1986

Answer Key:

1. 11%
2. straight from the can
3. on asparagus
4. 31%
5. 35%
6. 22
7. 24
8. 38

Nosy Rosy did a survey for the makers of Jumly, a brand-new food. She asked 200 people, "How do you eat your Jumly?" She put the results on a circle graph. Use the information from the graph to answer these questions on your paper. Check with the answer key.

1. What percentage of people eat Jumly in a sandwich?
2. How do most people surveyed eat their Jumly?
3. Do more people eat Jumly on asparagus or on waffles?
4. What percentage of people eat Jumly either on watermelon or ice cream?
5. What percentage of people eat Jumly either on waffles or from the can?

The whole graph represents the total number of people interviewed, 200 people or 100%. To find out how many people like Jumly straight from the can, multiply 200 by 26%.

0.26 x 200 = 52 people like Jumly from the can.

How many people like:

6. Jumly in a sandwich?
7. Jumly on ice cream?
8. Jumly on watermelon?

When Someone Mentions Vocabulary...

Try this novel approach to get your students to stick their necks out by using new vocabulary words. At the same time, they'll get practice in using a dictionary and in creative writing. Laminate folder, provide a wipe-off crayon, and change words frequently for a word to the wise.

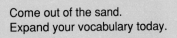

Come out of the sand.
Expand your vocabulary today.

Are these words new to you? Look each one up in a dictionary, and write a good definition in your own words. Then use each new word in a sentence to make its meaning clear:

New Word	Definition	Sentence

New Word	Definition	Sentence

IDEA!
Start your own collection of new words. Look in daily newspapers. Cut out words and glue them to paper in a special section of your vocabulary notebook.

When Someone Mentions Vocabulary...

Do You Feel Like Hiding?

Sandra Steen
Corinth, MS

Critical Consumers

Keep a file folder of magazine and newspaper advertisements. Have students sort them according to the type of "appeal" they use.

DIRECTIONS:
Sort these ads according to the list below:

1. Straightforward—just facts
2. Special Offer—coupon, prizes, etc.
3. Eye Appeal—looks good
4. Happy Family Appeal
5. Experts—claim it's good
6. Famous People's Testimonials
7. Bandwagon—Everybody buys it.
8. Snob Appeal—Not everybody can have it.
9. Youth Appeal—Kids like it.
10. Something New/Something's been added.
11. Statistics.

Critical Consumer

Sale   Special Offer $ $

save $ $

Ann Fausnight
Canton, OH

File Folder Ideas

1. Your uncle's mother's father's wife is what relation to you?
2. Your first cousin's uncle's mother is what relation to you?
3. Your aunt's father's only grandchild is what relation to you?
4. Your father's aunt's brother's wife is what relation to you?
5. Your first cousin's aunt's mother is what relation to you?
6. Your mother's uncle's brother's wife is what relation to you?
7. Your first cousin's aunt's father is what relation to you?
8. Your brother-in-law's mother-in-law's granddaughter is what relation to you?
9. Your father's mother's brother is what relation to you?
10. Your mother's mother's sister's husband is what relation to you?
11. Your mother's mother's son's son is what relation to you?
12. Your father's father's daughter's daughter is what relation to you?

Family Relations

Shake up the family tree with your students as you figure out these relationships. Students write answers on their own paper and check by the answer key.

NOTE TO TEACHER: This is an especially challenging one that you could use several different ways:

1. First define all relatives named so students understand relationships. Do activity together as a class, with students illustrating relationships by constructing a family tree on the chalkboard or overhead projector.
2. To have students work individually, suggest that they use paper and pencil to draw the family tree as stated.
3. Challenge academically gifted students with these problems. Then have them develop more problems to challenge other students.

Rebecca Webster Graves
Burlington, NC

Answer Key
1. great grandmother
2. grandmother (or not a relative)
3. yourself
4. grandmother/great aunt
5. grandmother (or not a relative)
6. grandmother/great aunt
7. grandfather (or not a relative)
8. niece/daughter
9. great uncle
10. great uncle
11. first cousin
12. first cousin

Crazy Face

There's never a loser in this zany math game! In addition to the file folder, you'll need to prepare 40–50 multiplication and division flash cards, two sets of face part cutouts, and a price list for the parts. Players earn cards to purchase face parts with, then make faces on the folder.

Kathy Gales
Tampa, FL

1. In turn, draw a card and give the answer.
2. Check the key and keep the card if correct.
3. When you have enough cards, use the price list to buy face parts. Place the cards you pay with at the bottom of the pile.
4. Game ends when all face parts have been bought.

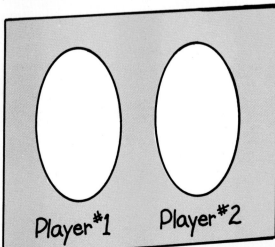

Player #1   Player #2

Eyes · 10 cards
Eyebrow · 5 cards
Nose · 8 cards
Ear · 2 cards
Mouth · 3 cards
Moustache · 6 cards

Wanted!

Place this just-for-fun file folder on a table equipped with large sheets of construction paper and markers. Students mount one of their school photos on construction paper, then write in the information listed in the folder. They use a stamp pad to add their fingerprints. Finished posters help students learn more about their classmates.

— Wanted —

Fingerprint

Mug Shot

Name: _____
Serial no: _____
Alias: _____
Address: _____
_____

Birthdate: day ____ month ____ yr. ____
Birthplace: _____
Age: ____ Weight: ____
Height: ____
Hair color: _____
Eyes: _____
Interests 1. _____
2. _____
Last seen: _____
Wearing: _____
Hanging around with: _____

Favorite subject: _____

Colors And Shapes

To make a challenging color and shape puzzle, you need four cutouts of each shape (circle, square, triangle, rectangle) in four colors (red, green, yellow, blue). Students arrange the cutouts on a file folder grid so that there is one of each color and shape in each row, both vertically and horizontally.

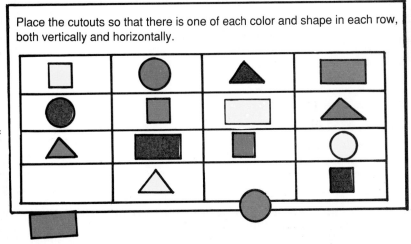

Place the cutouts so that there is one of each color and shape in each row, both vertically and horizontally.

Pick a pair and write some imaginary dialogue between them.

Pick A Pair

Thanksgiving Dialogue

In a file folder offer these creative ideas for writing some imaginary dialogues between the following pairs:

The captain of the *Mayflower* and a seasick sailor
A turkey and a Pilgrim with a hatchet
Two Pilgrims who thought they knew their way back to camp
Two Pilgrims unable to successfully cut down a tree

from Holiday Center Ideas by Judy Streb and Ann Heflin

Christmas Pinwheel Wreath

Your students will be delighted with the finished product of this following-directions folder. Place all materials in a convenient center. Display completed wreaths in your room. You may wish to demonstrate the directions to your class before letting your students try it individually.

Claudia Vurnakes
Summerfield, NC

Make a pinwheel wreath!

You need:

a pencil
a ruler
green construction paper
scissors
a stapler
4" cardboard square

cardboard (10" square)
a compass
glue
red construction paper
red ribbon

How To Make:

1. Trace ten 4-inch squares on the green construction paper. Cut them out.
2. Cut each square on the dotted lines.

 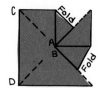

3. Fold marked corners in to the center. Staple in the middle.

4. On the 10" cardboard, draw 2 circles, one 10" in diameter and another 6 inches in diameter.

5. Cut along the lines you have drawn. Now you have the base for your wreath.

6. Glue each pinwheel onto the base.

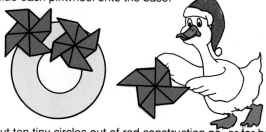

7. Cut ten tiny circles out of red construction paper for berries.
8. Glue a berry in the center of each pinwheel.
9. Tie a ribbon at the bottom of your wreath and hang it up!

Last-Minute Shopping

Wind up your Christmas preparations with an addition/multiplication file folder. Students find the cost for each item on the shopping list, then find the total cost. The correct total is $3,321.00!

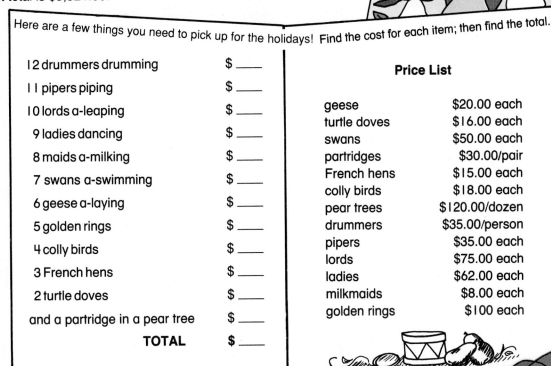

Here are a few things you need to pick up for the holidays! Find the cost for each item; then find the total.

12 drummers drumming	$ ___
11 pipers piping	$ ___
10 lords a-leaping	$ ___
9 ladies dancing	$ ___
8 maids a-milking	$ ___
7 swans a-swimming	$ ___
6 geese a-laying	$ ___
5 golden rings	$ ___
4 colly birds	$ ___
3 French hens	$ ___
2 turtle doves	$ ___
and a partridge in a pear tree	$ ___
TOTAL	$ ___

Price List

geese	$20.00 each
turtle doves	$16.00 each
swans	$50.00 each
partridges	$30.00/pair
French hens	$15.00 each
colly birds	$18.00 each
pear trees	$120.00/dozen
drummers	$35.00/person
pipers	$35.00 each
lords	$75.00 each
ladies	$62.00 each
milkmaids	$8.00 each
golden rings	$100 each

Holiday Theme Words

Use this folder year-round to celebrate every holiday season. Cut a slit in the folder, insert a paper clip, and attach the word list. Change the words when the next special season rolls around.

Rebecca Webster Graves
Burlington, NC

1. List the words in alphabetical order.

2. Write the number of syllables in each word.

3. Make a sentence with five of the words.

4. Write the definitions of any three words.

5. Draw a picture illustrating four of the words.

6. Write a story using all of the words.

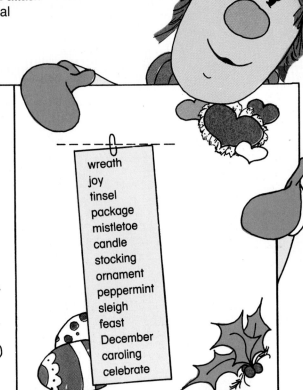

wreath
joy
tinsel
package
mistletoe
candle
stocking
ornament
peppermint
sleigh
feast
December
caroling
celebrate

File Folder Ideas

True Love

Charm your students with these loving snakes. Draw artwork in the folder and add two pockets. Write true/false social studies or science statements on cards. Provide an answer key if desired. To vary, make cards and pockets for correct/incorrect, fact/opinion, or greater/less than skills.

Rebecca G. Simpson
Winston-Salem, NC

The capital of Spain is Madrid.

Place each heart in the correct pocket.

True

False

Heartaches By The Number

Have students spin to find equivalents. Cut out paper hearts and heart halves. Every time a child spins two fractions of equivalent value, he gets a heart. "Heartaches" (spins that don't match) are awarded a broken heart. Five broken hearts may be turned in for one heart. The winner has the most hearts after ten spins. Provide a chart of equivalents as an answer key.

1. In turn, spin each spinner.
2. If the fractions or decimals are equivalent, take a heart.
3. If the fractions or decimals are not equivalent, take a broken heart. You may exchange five broken hearts for a whole heart.
4. Be sure to check your answers with the key.
5. The winner has the most hearts after ten spins.

Answer Key					
$\frac{1}{2}$	.50	$\frac{50}{100}$	$\frac{6}{12}$	$\frac{2}{4}$	$\frac{18}{36}$
$\frac{1}{4}$	.25	$\frac{25}{100}$	$\frac{8}{32}$	$\frac{10}{40}$	
$\frac{3}{4}$	.75	$\frac{75}{100}$	$\frac{9}{12}$	$\frac{27}{36}$	

A Touch Of Irish Luck

This list of words will generate lots of creative writing from your students. Cut out the worksheet below and glue it inside a file folder. (You may wish to duplicate page 36 before doing this step.) Encourage children to add more words and illustrations as they think of them. Vary with additional language arts activities and additional folders for other holidays.

Do Number 1. Then choose three more activities. Do them on your own paper.

1. Make up a story using at least ten of these words.

2. List the words in alphabetical order.

3. Find five of the words in a dictionary. Write the guide words and a definition for each one.

4. List the words by the number of syllables.

5. Use a thesaurus to find synonyms for five of the words.

6. Match each word to its part(s) of speech.

7. Make a word search on graph paper. Hide at least 12 of these words horizontally, vertically, and diagonally in it. Provide an answer key.

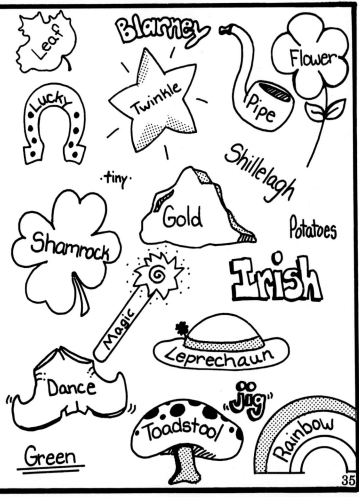

RAINY DAY ACTIVITIES

Pop-up Invitations

Send these clever invitations to your Open House. Parents will find a surprise inside. The directions may sound complicated at first, but with the teacher demonstrating, even first graders can handle this project with great success.

Wendy Sondov
Montclair, NJ

Materials Needed: 9" x 12" construction paper, scissors, crayons

Directions:

1. Hold paper vertically. Fold in half, left to right. Make a crisp crease.
2. Fold the paper in half again, this time from top to bottom. Make a crisp crease; then open the paper as it was in step one.
3. Along the folded edge, make a one-inch cut about one to two inches down from the center crease.
4. Fold back the cut edges to form two triangles. Be sure all creases are crisp.
5. Open paper fully; then refold into a card shape. The pop-up feature should open when the card is opened, but you may need to gently pry the paper up the first time it is used.
6. Draw a creature inside the card to fit the pop-up mouth or eye, and write a greeting.

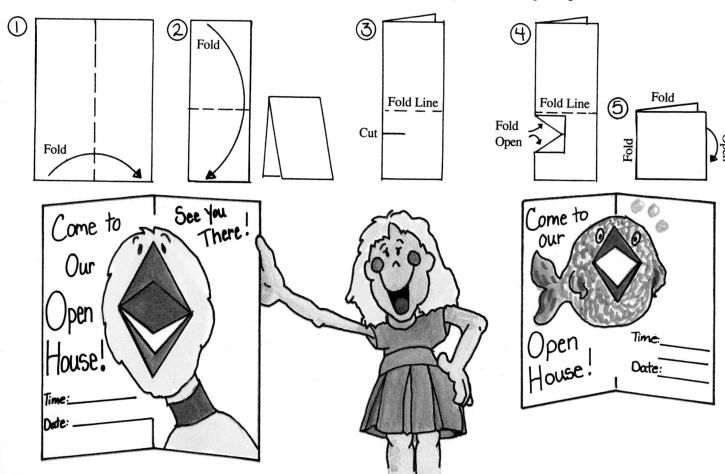

Steps for making:

1. Cut off the tops of 10–12 small, unpeeled apples and slice horizontally. Slices should be approximately 1/8-inch thick.

2. Place slices on a wire rack or window screen to dry until leathery. (Allow about two weeks for drying.)

3. Attach a piece of Styrofoam oasis (used in floral arrangements) to the end of a length of heavy florist wire or a coat hanger. This will keep slices from falling out during stringing.

4. Gently run the wire through the center of the apple slices. Alternate slices with inexpensive dried flowers. Glue the flowers to the slices with small amounts of rubber cement.

5. After stringing, bend to form a wreath. Attach ends together and cut off excess wire.

6. Add a touch of country ribbon to finish.

For smaller, individual wreaths, use 5–6 apples per child.

Country Wreaths

Bring a bit of country charm into your classroom with a wreath-making project. Organize students in small groups to construct their wreaths. Enlist the help of several parent volunteers if possible.

Diana West
Big Horn, WV

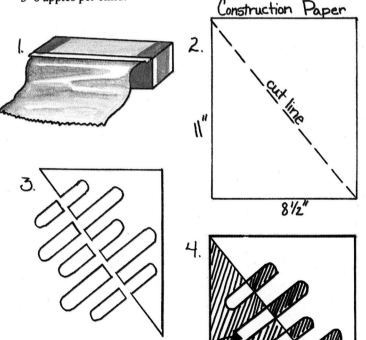

Mirror Images

Hang these "mirrors" for shiny reflections. Students receive 8 1/2" x 11" pieces of aluminum foil. These are glued onto pieces of lightweight cardboard. Cut 8 1/2" x 11" sheets of colored construction paper in half or on the diagonal. Students cut designs along the center edge and flip cut-out pieces over. Pieces are glued to the foil close to the construction paper edge for a mirror image. Try faces, symbols, flags, and seasonal images.

Sr. Ann Claire Rhoads
Emmitsburg, MD

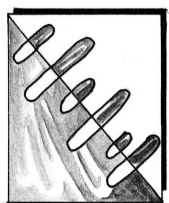

RAINY DAY ACTIVITIES

crease

crease   crease

Easy Picture Frames

Take a sheet of construction paper and crease each corner in about one inc diagonally. Very gently, fold up the sides. (Do not crease.) Place children's a or work papers inside. Makes an attractive bulletin board for displaying stude art.

Lois Cooper
Beckley, WV

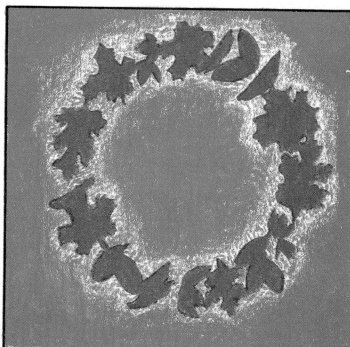

Spray Paint Silhouettes

After students have collected leaves, seed pods, and grasses, have them arrange the items in a circular pattern on white paper. Use rubber cement to tack them down. Spray the entire paper with a colored paint. When dry, remove the leaves and paint the white areas with a contrasting color.

Marcia Backstrom
Bethel Park, PA

Crayon Shaving Mosaics

Sometimes, substituting a different art medium is all that's needed to create a great, new art project. How about using crayon shavings to fill in a mosaic picture? Save crayon "nubs" and shave them with a sharpener. Have students glue colored shavings to original watercolor paintings or designs outlined with colored markers. The combined use of media makes an outstanding impression!

Sr. Ann Claire Rhoads
Emmitsburg, MD

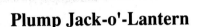

Colored Salt On Foil

Your students will want to show off these sparkling art projects. Begin by putting some salt in a plastic bag, adding a few drops of paint, and shaking until well mixed. Allow the salt mixture to dry; then crumble any chunks. Create several different colors in this manner and store them in old salt shakers. Have each student cover a piece of cardboard with aluminum foil. Students draw glue lines on the foil and shake on colored salt. Completed projects may be framed by gluing on a rickrack border.

Sr. Ann Claire Rhoads
Emmitsburg, MD

Plump Jack-o'-Lantern

This jack-o'-lantern looks like the real thing! To begin, stack ten 1" x 9" strips of orange paper in a pile. Use a paper punch to carefully punch a matching hole at both ends of each strip. Next add a 1" x 2" piece of green construction paper (stem) to the pile, with a matching hole. Fasten each end of the pile with a paper fastener. Spread the strips apart to form a sphere, bending the stem up. Use construction paper scraps and glue on a jack-o'-lantern face. Add curled green ribbon for vines. Hang from the ceiling or display on tabletops.

Lois Benedict
White Bear Lake, MN

Crayon Shaving Turkeys

Cut a turkey body from brown paper and place on a sheet of waxed paper. Sprinkle crayon shavings where the feathers would be. Cover with another sheet of waxed paper, then newsprint, and iron. Attach black paper strips to the top and bottom, punch holes in the top, and hang with yarn.

Marilyn Edman
Warren, MN

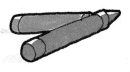

Make A Christmas Village

Trace or reproduce the pattern on heavy paper. Then decorate with store signs, windows, fancy doors, etc. To make a warehouse or church, add 1/2 inch at the bottom. For a one-story house, subtract one inch at the bottom. Cut on solid lines, fold on dotted lines, and paste together.

Shirley Liby
Muncie, IN

Pretzel Wreaths

Make a unique gift for someone special. Place six large pretzels in a circle. Glue six pretzels on top, staggering the bottom row. After the glue dries, weave two-inch ribbon through the wreath and tie a bow. Attach holly or a colorful decoration.

Debbie Wiggins
Myrtle Beach, SC

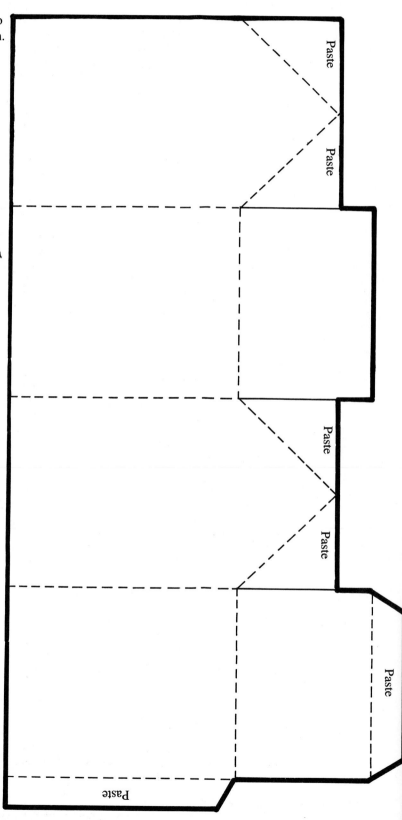

Santa Pencil Topper

Cute Santa pencil toppers will get everyone in the holiday spirit! Duplicate the patterns below for each child. The student cuts out pieces from felt or construction paper and follows the steps given. These make nice gifts or party favors to give to younger children.

Jayne Petrea
Gold Hill, NC

Santa Pencil Topper

1. Cut one of each pattern.
2. Glue beard to face.
3. Glue on nose.
4. Glue on hat, trim, and then the white ball.
5. Add details shown in bold with black, fine-tipped marker.
6. Glue front to back with a pencil in the middle.

Finished Topper

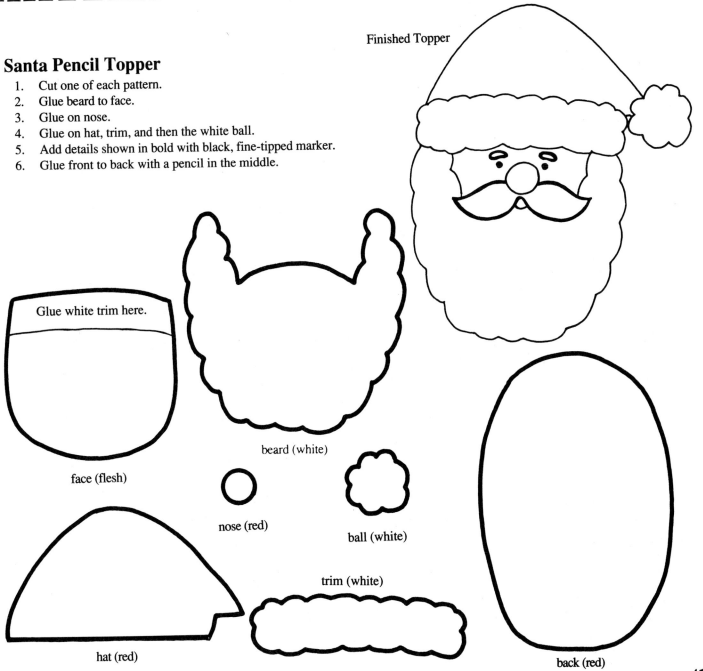

Glue white trim here.

face (flesh)

beard (white)

nose (red)

ball (white)

trim (white)

hat (red)

back (red)

Class Christmas Tree

Brighten your classroom door with an eye-catching Christmas tree. Have each student paint a Styrofoam cup green. (Depending on the number of students in your class, you may need a few extra cups to complete the tree shape.) Students use the bottom of the cup to trace a small round picture from an old Christmas card. After cutting out the circle, the student glues it inside the bottom of his cup. For sparkle, let students dip the cup mouth in glue, then in glitter. Glue all the cups on a large, tagboard triangular tree. Post on your classroom door.

Sr. Ann Claire Rhoads
Emmitsburg, MD

acetate

Stained Glass Art

To make these pretty stained glass pictures, place a 9" x 12" piece of acetate over a Christmas picture and trace with a permanent marker. Use crayons to color in, pressing hard. (Nancy has her kids work in pairs to help hold each other's pictures.) Wad a piece of aluminum foil (a little larger than 9" x 12") into a loose ball and smooth out flat. Lay the acetate, color side down, on the foil and place on a piece of 9" x 12" cardboard. Using masking tape, tape all four sides on the cardboard to form a frame. Color the tape with markers or leave plain.

aluminum foil

Nancy Kochsmeier
San Diego, CA

masking tape

Champagne Glass Ornaments

Plastic champagne glasses work best with this project, but tumblers can also be used. After removing the bases of two champagne glasses, use a sharp compass point to poke a hole through each stem end. Fill with dried flowers, colorful ribbons or yarn, or tissue paper. Fit the rims together and secure with decorative tape. Attach a yarn or tinsel tassel in the bottom hole, and insert a paper clip hanger into the top hole.

Sylvia McFeaters
Slippery Rock, PA

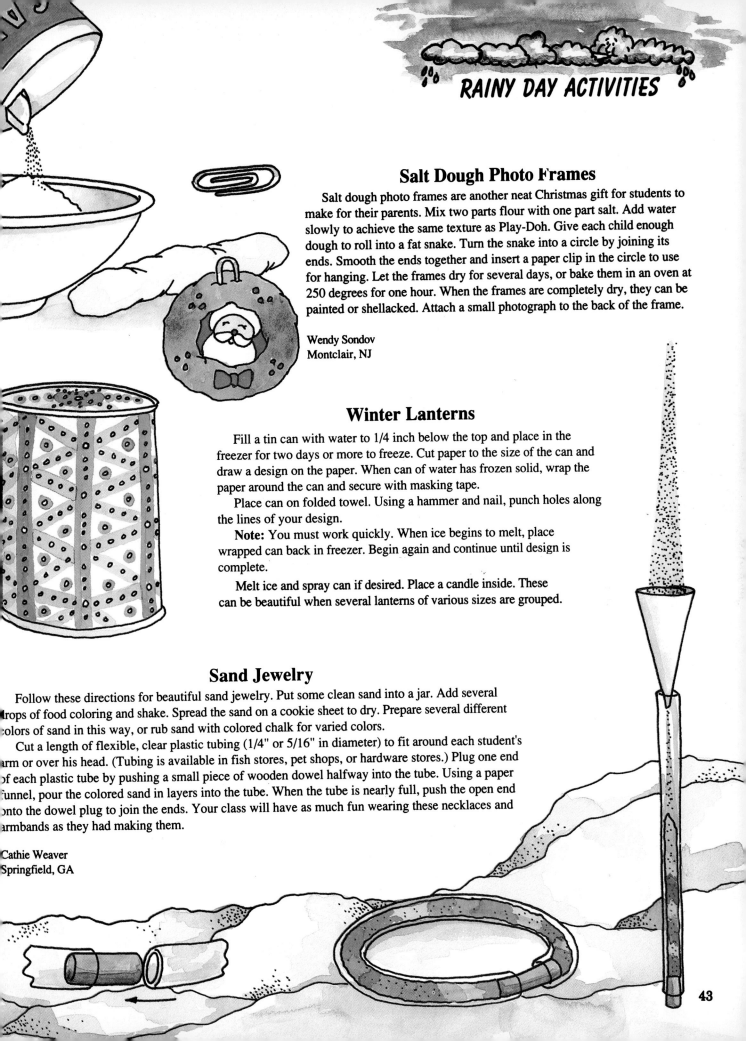

Salt Dough Photo Frames

Salt dough photo frames are another neat Christmas gift for students to make for their parents. Mix two parts flour with one part salt. Add water slowly to achieve the same texture as Play-Doh. Give each child enough dough to roll into a fat snake. Turn the snake into a circle by joining its ends. Smooth the ends together and insert a paper clip in the circle to use for hanging. Let the frames dry for several days, or bake them in an oven at 250 degrees for one hour. When the frames are completely dry, they can be painted or shellacked. Attach a small photograph to the back of the frame.

Wendy Sondov
Montclair, NJ

Winter Lanterns

Fill a tin can with water to 1/4 inch below the top and place in the freezer for two days or more to freeze. Cut paper to the size of the can and draw a design on the paper. When can of water has frozen solid, wrap the paper around the can and secure with masking tape.

Place can on folded towel. Using a hammer and nail, punch holes along the lines of your design.

Note: You must work quickly. When ice begins to melt, place wrapped can back in freezer. Begin again and continue until design is complete.

Melt ice and spray can if desired. Place a candle inside. These can be beautiful when several lanterns of various sizes are grouped.

Sand Jewelry

Follow these directions for beautiful sand jewelry. Put some clean sand into a jar. Add several drops of food coloring and shake. Spread the sand on a cookie sheet to dry. Prepare several different colors of sand in this way, or rub sand with colored chalk for varied colors.

Cut a length of flexible, clear plastic tubing (1/4" or 5/16" in diameter) to fit around each student's arm or over his head. (Tubing is available in fish stores, pet shops, or hardware stores.) Plug one end of each plastic tube by pushing a small piece of wooden dowel halfway into the tube. Using a paper funnel, pour the colored sand in layers into the tube. When the tube is nearly full, push the open end onto the dowel plug to join the ends. Your class will have as much fun wearing these necklaces and armbands as they had making them.

Cathie Weaver
Springfield, GA

RAINY DAY ACTIVITIES

Broken Hearts

Draw and cut out a large heart. Cut the heart into pieces. Put them back together again on a background of a different color, leaving a small space between each piece.

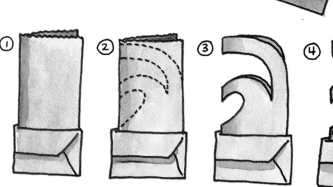

Valentine Bags

Treat your students to a special valentine sack. With the sack flat, fold it vertically along the center. Cut a handle at the top. Snip some heart decorations. Add to the cut design by using a paper punch. Decorate with markers, cut paper, stickers, or crayons. Personalize each sack with the student's name.

Shirley Liby
Muncie, IN

Valentine Mailboxes For The School

Thinking of sending a valentine to a special someone at your school, but alas, they have no mailbox? Your students can solve this dilemma, and ensure that the entire school staff is remembered on Valentine's Day. As a class project, have groups of students construct mailboxes for the librarian, school counselor, school nurse, teaching specialists, bus drivers, and cafeteria, office, and custodial workers.

Ask children to make an alphabetical listing of all of the school personnel. Duplicate the list for other classes. Before Valentine's Day, your class can make heart-shaped name tags for these special people. This will help children to identify those familiar faces by name when they write their valentines. The whole school will take notice!

Then have student groups cover grocery boxes with aluminum foil. Students decorate the boxes by gluing tissue-paper hearts to the foil and adding the appropriate staff name or names. Place the mailboxes in the school lobby or other convenient location so that students from all classes can drop in their valentines.

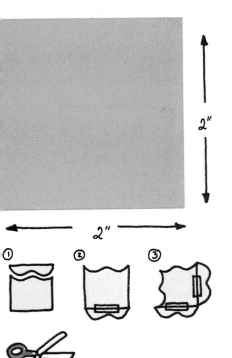

2"

2"

Tessellated Designs

Creating these unique mosaic patterns is an art project with a math-concept bonus. Each student will need a two-inch square of construction paper and a 12" x 18" sheet of white art paper.

Procedure:

1. Create negative space by cutting a free-form shape from one side of a two-inch square.
2. Tape that piece to the opposite side of the square to create positive space.
3. Repeat steps one and two with the other sides. (While the paper is no longer a square, it has the same area.)
4. Use the irregular shape as a template and trace onto art paper. Repeat the design by fitting the template against the first outline and tracing. Continue tracing the design to fill the paper.
5. Using two colors, color alternating spaces.

Melissa Matusevich
Blacksburg, VA

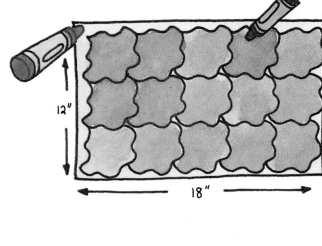

12"

18"

Dipped Carnations

Here's an old idea with a new twist. Unfold a facial tissue and tear in half lengthwise. Repeat this step and stack all four sections. Tear off smooth edges for a rippled effect. Pleat and secure with a green pipe cleaner. Gently separate the folds. Then dip the flower edges in a solution containing equal parts of water and food coloring. Bend the pipe cleaner to form a hook, and hang upside down to dry.

Cindy Newell
Durant, OK

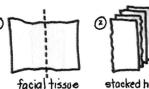

facial tissue   stacked halves

Straight From The Heart

Get wrapped up in these laced, heartfelt surprises. First, children cut two construction paper hearts, decorating one side of each with drawings or written messages. Holding hearts together, each student uses a paper punch to make holes along the edges. Students lace the hearts together with colorful ribbon. Stuff with tissue paper and wrapped candy or gum before finishing the lacing and tying a bow.

Lucille Jonston
Golden, CO

45

Noodle Nests

Try this easy recipe for an Eastertime project.
You will need:
   1 can chocolate frosting
   4 cups chow mein noodles
   Jelly beans

Heat the frosting over low heat and stir until liquid. Remove from heat and stir in the noodles. Drop by 1/4 cupfuls onto a cookie sheet; then press the centers in with a spoon to form nests. Add jelly beans and let set until firm.

Elaine Belscher
Spring Hill, FL

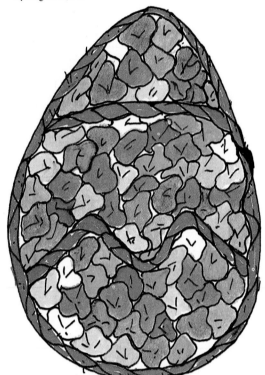

Tissue Paper Eggs

These colorful, textured eggs can be used to make a beautiful bulletin board. Glue yarn on construction paper eggs to outline and divide them into sections. Using different colors, ball up small pieces of tissue paper and fill in the sections. Glue them in place, making attractive designs.

Bunny Bleich
Tucson, AZ

Fresh Spring Hyacinths

Your classroom will bloom with these spring flowers. Each child needs an empty toilet paper roll, glue, 1 1/2-inch squares of purple and pink tissue paper, a pencil, green construction paper, scissors, floral tape, and a plastic straw. Staple one end of the toilet paper roll, and cut it to a rounded shape. Cover tube completely with tissue squares applied by folding, one at a time, over the end of a pencil and dabbing lightly in glue. Add construction paper leaves and a stem made from a plastic straw wound with floral tape. Plant these in cups or on a bulletin board.

Carol R. Witherell
Westfield, MA

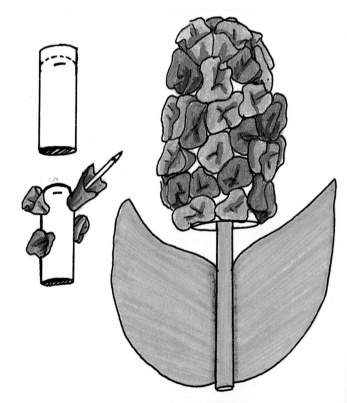

Adorable Bunnies

These terry cloth bunnies are a simple craft project and an ideal Easter treat or party favor. You will need washcloths, ribbon, and wiggle eyes to make these bunnies.

1. Roll two opposite corners of an old washcloth to the center.
2. Fold in half, keeping the rolls on the outside.
3. Fold the two loose ends back.
4. Tie with a ribbon and glue on wiggle eyes.
5. To use as a party favor, tuck a plastic, treat-filled egg into the body portion of the bunny.

Cathie Weaver
Springfield, GA

Mother's Day Sachets

Create these three-dimensional sachets to freshen up any drawer or room. Mom will love it!

Materials:

cardboard hearts
glue
scissors
perfume
yarn
felt
cotton balls
fabric
ribbon or lace
pencil or pen

Procedure:

1. Trace a heart shape onto two pieces of felt.
2. Cut the center out of one felt heart to make a window.
3. Put a few drops of perfume on a cotton ball. Glue the cotton to the center of the whole heart.
4. Glue a piece of fabric over the cotton.
5. Position a yarn loop between the felt hearts, and glue the two hearts together.
6. Add ribbon or lace for decorations.
7. Give it to your mother to hang in her closet.

Connie Harper
Parishville, NY

RAINY DAY ACTIVITIES

Mother's Day Promise Nosegay

Have children write promises on strips of paper. Fold each strip neatly. Put promise in center of tissue paper (4" x 4") and gather ends of tissue to form a flow Put bunch of flowers together. Insert in doily. Add green leaves with foil over ster Tie with a pretty bow.

Fran Petersen
North Tonawanda, NY

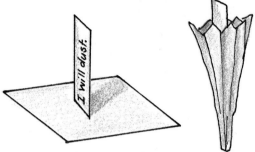

Plastic Soda Bottles

Here are two ideas using large, two-liter plastic bottles:

Use a heated ice pick to make three holes near the upper part of the bottle. Fill with water to just below the holes; then place philodendron in the holes. Put the cap back on and hang at the top with a nylon cord.

Dorothy Simmons
Memphis, TN

Remove the bottom from a bottle, and fill with soil and small plants. Cut off the top of the bottle as shown and place over the plants for a miniature terrarium.

Brenda Frank
Mt. View, OK

Remove black end from bottom. →

Cut here

Discard

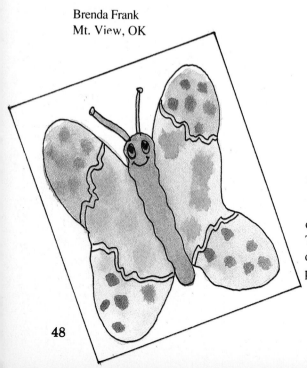

Wet On Wet

Draw a faint outline of a butterfly on a piece of paper. Wet the paper and lay it fla on a table. Choose pastels or bright colors of paint, and touch the wet paper lightly. The colors will spread into beautiful designs. Let the paper dry *thoroughly*. When it i dry, add black lines of paint with a fine-tip brush. Using the brush handle for the blac paint gives an interesting effect.

48

Borrowers' Club

Have trouble with students borrowing pencils and paper? Start a Borrowers' Club. Each student puts in 25 sheets of paper and two new pencils to join. When a student runs out, he may borrow up to the amount he paid in. To regain the borrowing privilege, the student must rejoin with more paper and pencils.

LaDonna Hauser
Wilmington, NC

Treasure Hunt

Have a treasure hunt to get your classroom cleaned that last day of school! Divide students into teams of three to four members each. Write clues on paper and hide them around the room, making several clues for each group. Each clue should direct finders to the next clue. The last clue might send students to the cafeteria for an ice cream treat!

Nancy Greeley
Hopkins, MO

Clue 1: Take down math bulletin board. Check with teacher before going to Clue 2. Go to Lisa's chair for Clue 2.

Clue 2: Wash desk tops on first three rows. Check with teacher before going to Clue 3.

Student ID Numbers

In order to quickly see whose work is missing and to record grades rapidly, give each student an identification number. Assign numbers to a name list alphabetized by last names. Students write their names and numbers on all work. When collecting papers, place them in numerical order. Instead of looking for a name in your roll book, go down the ID number list.

Helene Croft
Chatsworth, CA

Good Work Reward

Promote good study habits. Before a big test, give each student a list of points to study. At the bottom, explain that a parent or older sibling may sign the paper to show that the student studied at home. A passing test grade with a signed study sheet earns a special reward. It really works!

Jan Drehmel
Chippewa Falls, WI

The Loan Solution

When loaning *Mailbox* issues, I ask each teacher to write her name and the issue she is borrowing on a piece of ditto paper. She places the paper in the spot from which she took the magazine. I can quickly tell who has the issue I need.

Mary Dinneen
Bristol, CT

Coding With Colored Dots

Use assorted colored dots to code file folder activities, games, Pocket Pals, and learning centers. Using the code, children can see at a glance the maximum number of students who may use the activity at one time.

Code:
red dot—1 student   orange dot—2 students
green dot—3 students

Cathie Weaver
Springfield, GA

Did It Go In The Grade Book?

My fourth graders were constantly wanting to know which daily papers were recorded in my grade book. Now they know at a glance. I simply cut the corners off all papers that I record.

Jenny Camarata
Athens, TN

Make-up Work

Take the headache out of make-up work with this clever idea. Label and laminate a file folder. Mount the folder in a place students frequently visit, such as directly above the pencil sharpener. Appoint a student volunteer to label and place the work for absent students in the file folder. When the absent students return, they check the file folder for their make-up work. This folder is also very handy when parents or friends stop by for work.

Ruby Pesek
Lake Jackson, TX

49

Lifesavers

School Supplies

Be prepared when ordering time rolls around this year. Keep an index card in your desk drawer, and write down needed items as they come to mind. When it's time to place your order, you'll have your list of reminders.

Mary Dinneen
Bristol, CT

Organizing Lesson Plans

Eliminate those last-minute struggles to collect materials for lessons. Label five folders "Monday" through "Friday." While writing lesson plans, highlight the extra supplies needed for each day. Stock each folder with the necessary supplies.

Sharleen Berg
Jefferson, SD

Substitute Saver

This little idea can save your next substitute teacher a lot of headaches. In your plans, suggest that she offer 15 extra minutes of recess at the end of the day if students maintain good behavior. Students are usually motivated by this proposition and will work hard for the opportunity to spend more time outside.

Robert Kinker
Bexley, OH

Every Month Calendar

Make a calendar you can use every month, every year! Cut eight cardboard strips and label as shown. Pin the weekday strip in place; then position the correct date column under the first day of the current month. Arrange the other date columns accordingly. Presto—a calendar that's easy and fun to update!

JeNan Merrill
Columbia, TN

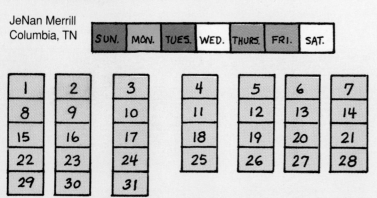

Holiday Helpers

Encourage your students to pass on the holid spirit by starting a "Santa's Helpers" club. Let studer sign up to help any teacher in your school who nee an extra hand in setting up projects, tutoring, e Before a helper is allowed to assist a teacher, he mu have exhibited good behavior during the day and ha completed all required work.

Helene Sparaco
Middleburgh, NY

End-of-the-Day Reminders

Do you sometimes forget some of the things yo should remind students of at the end of the day? Wri "Don't Forget" at the top of a sheet of constructio paper. Laminate the paper and tape it to the inside your classroom door. During the day, as you think things that students will need to be reminded of, j them on the paper with a wipe-off marker. At the end each day, refer to the "Don't Forget" reminder befo sending the students home.

Mary Beltz
Gillette, WY

HELP!

During a class period when children are working individualized activities, print the word HELP on th blackboard. Students can then sign up on the board they need teacher assistance. Ask students who sig up to put the troublesome page numbers by thei names so that you can help several students with th same problem together.

Cathy Schreiber
Redondo Beach, CA

Point Bank

Students in my science and health classes ar motivated by our "point bank." Students earn points b bringing in things needed for class and newspaper c magazine articles about a current topic of study, or b answering the "point question" correctly. The poin question is asked at the beginning of a class period. pertains directly to the previous night's readin assignment and can be answered in one word. Point accumulated in the point bank may be added to homework grade to improve it.

Norma Stephan
Allegany, NY

Puzzle Poster

This is the best management tool I've ever used! Mount an animal or bird poster on tagboard and laminate. Laminate a second piece of tagboard of the same size and cut into puzzle pieces; then number each piece. Cover the poster by attaching puzzle pieces with double-faced sticky tape or rubber cement. Call on a student seated at the quietest table to remove a piece and guess what's on the poster. A correct guess earns a treat for the entire group. Works well for times when you want to settle students—after recess, between classes, or waiting for buses at the end of the day. As the poster becomes clearer, children become very eager to earn a guess!

Diane Lucas
Pittsburgh, PA

Photo Find

Looking for a creative way to divide students into study groups? Find one large magazine photograph for each group you wish to form. Cut each photograph into four, five, or six pieces. Mix up the pieces. As each student enters the room, give him a piece of a photograph. On your signal, students try to reassemble each photo by locating the other pieces. The students whose pieces make up a photograph become a study group.

Sr. Ann Claire Rhoads
Emmitsburg, MD

Lesson Plan Reminders

Here's an easy way to stay on top of upcoming events. Jot information down on a stick-on note and place it in your plan book on the appropriate date. You'll be pleasantly reminded of the event when you complete your plans for that week.

Vail Neal
Cleveland, MS

Easiest Seating Chart

Use small Post-it™ notes and oaktag to make the easiest seating chart ever. Write each child's name on a small note and place it in position on the oaktag. Tape a transparent sheet over the seating chart. When students change seats, simply lift the transparency and reposition the notes.

Mary Dinneen
Bristol, CT

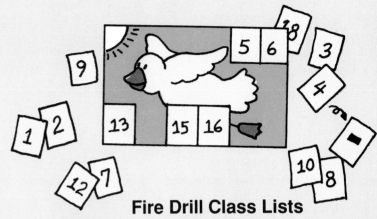

Fire Drill Class Lists

When the fire drill alarm rings, I am unwilling to take valuable time to locate my attendance book to carry with me. However, I need an accurate list of my class so I can take attendance and be sure no one is overlooked. At the beginning of the school year, I make class lists of all classes that meet in my room. I mark it "Fire Drill Class Lists" and tape it to my doorway. When the fire alarm rings, I take it down and carry it along.

Peggy Neubauer
Parma, OH

Spelling Graphs

To increase student responsibility and decrease record-keeping, keep a Spelling Grade folder with a graph sheet for each student. Prepare the graph sheets so that the children themselves can record the number of correct words on their weekly spelling tests. Eliminates some of your grading work with an added bonus—the students get a chance to practice graphing!

Susan Chisari
Orlando, FL

Attendance Chains

Encourage good attendance by making a chain of colored construction paper links. Add a link every day all the students are present. Set a perfect attendance goal of a certain number of days, and with the students, plan some type of reward: an extra recess, free time, a party, etc. As the chain grows longer, the students get excited and encourage one another to achieve the attendance goal. Once the goal has been achieved, begin working on a new chain and a new attendance record.

Gail Cooper
Grayslake, IL

Save Those Cards!

Save old cards, new cards, holiday cards, get well cards and birthday cards. There are countless ways to use them.

Rebecca Webster Graves
Burlington, NC

- For puppets, cut animals, people, or things from cards. Add paper rings for finger puppets. Use Popsicle sticks or toothpicks for stick puppets.
- Clip corner borders for bulletin board or gameboard decorations.
- Cut characters or objects from cards. Then give to students who glue them on paper and complete a scene.

- Sort cards according to type, and make a graph showing the number in each category.

Roses are red.
Violets are blue.
Sugar is sweet
But not as
sweet as you.

- Cut off the inside verses from cards. Use the rest to stimulate students to write:

  —riddles   —jokes   —limericks
  —stories   —poems   —original verses

  —alliteration or tongue twisters to accompany pictures
  —advertisements—Be sure to encourage the use of descriptive words.
  —sentences or a paragraph describing what's on the card
  —a character description of a person or animal on the card
  —lists of everything in the picture— Kids enjoy making lists!
  —nursery rhymes written by older students for younger ones
  —haiku to accompany nature scenes on cards

- To make a book of student writings, cut extra sheets the size of cards, insert pages, and staple.
- Use cards with text intact for students to identify the parts of speech of words.
- Use a picture from a card to develop a group story. Students pass the card, and each one adds a sentence. If desired, record the sentences on chart paper.

Round off the total to the nearest dollar.

Arrange the prices from least to greatest.

Check It Out!

Save those register tapes from the grocery store for real-life math lessons. Number or color code the receipts, and place them at a center with these task cards:

1. Round off the total to the nearest dollar.
2. Figure change from a $100 bill.
3. Write three word problems using the numbers on your tape. Find the answers. Show your work.
4. Subtract rebates and coupons from the total.
5. Find the total tax. Add to the subtotal to find the total spent.
6. Cut the sales slip into groups of ten or less items. Find the average cost per item.
7. Arrange prices from least to greatest.
8. Write the total in words.

Janice Scott
Rockport, TX

The NFL Today

Look forward to fall with this football center. Make a wall poster in the shape of the NFL shield. List the teams in each division and make two slots after each team's name. Use Tuesday's sports section to post win-loss records for each team in the first slots. A team of students computes the winning percentage for each team and these are posted in the second slots. You'll be surprised at the enthusiasm this exercise generates.

Ann Price Friedman
Birmingham, AL

NFL WEST

ATLANTA	10-2	.833
SAN FRANCISCO	8-4	
LOS ANGELES	6-6	
NEW ORLEANS	4-8	

The Creative Learning Center

Turn an old teacher's desk into a creative learning center. Fill the desk drawers with tools such as pens, pencils, crayons, markers, a variety of paper, scissors, and glue. On the desktop, place research materials to stimulate writing ideas, projects, and activities. Tack a piece of white paper inside the chair opening to make a viewing area for filmstrips and slides. Label baskets with "Work in Progress," "Completed Activities," and "Help Needed," and place with a checklist to help keep track of student work.

Robert A. DiSibio and Linda Ulmer
Philadelphia, PA

Handwriting Center

If you have an old student tabletop desk, you've got the makings of an unusual handwriting center. Cover the desktop with lined chart paper. Then place clear Con-Tact paper over it for protection. Students use washable markers to practice handwriting activities written on index cards. Provide Handi-wipes for quick, easy cleanup. Each desk job is a favorite with student writers.

Kathy Barrow
Orange Park, FL

Puzzle Maps

Cut maps from old geography books or atlases into 10–15 puzzle pieces, and place in an envelope. (You may want to mount the map on poster board and laminate before cutting.) Write five questions regarding the map on the outside of the envelope. The pupils put the map together and answer the questions.

Sylvia McFeaters
Slippery Rock, PA

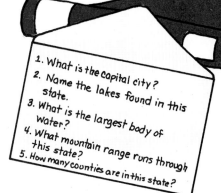

1. What is the capital city?
2. Name the lakes found in this state.
3. What is the largest body of water?
4. What mountain range runs through this state?
5. How many counties are in this state?

Web Spinners

Players choose four red or four black spiders and place each in the starting positions. In turn, each student draws a prefix card and checks the first word in all four of his paths. If the prefix can be added correctly to any one of the words, the player moves his spider up. No jumping of words is allowed. Play continues until a player gets one spider home!

Kathi Kiger
Greensboro, NC

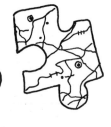

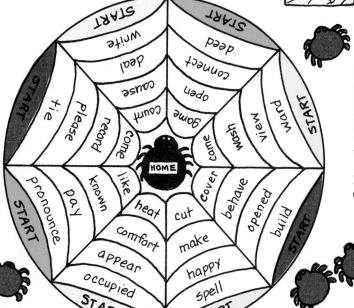

pre- re- in-

mis- dis- un- be-

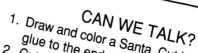

Can We Talk?

Here's a writing center worth talking about! Ask students to bring in old magazines containing pictures of famous personalities. Place the magazines at a center with a supply of tongue depressors (two per student). When all students have completed the center, schedule a sharing time when student puppeteers can present their conversations.

Jane Theoharides
Lincoln, ME

CAN WE TALK?

1. Draw and color a Santa. Cut him out and glue to the end of a tongue depressor.
2. Cut out a magazine picture of a famous person. Glue to another tongue depressor.
3. Write a conversation between Santa and your famous person. Use correct punctuation and capitalization. Be creative!
4. Practice reading your conversation using your puppets.

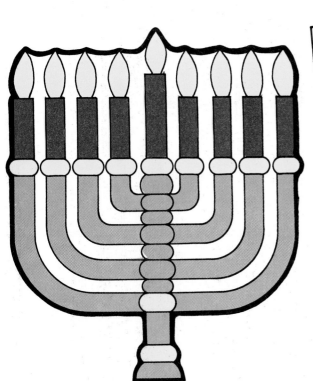

Swiftly <u>he</u> ran from the burning house.

pronoun

Light The Menorah

To prepare this parts-of-speech game, provide each player with a poster board menorah and eight cut-out flames. (See the menorah pattern on page 25.)

Label a set of cards with sentences in which one word is underlined. In turn, players draw a card and identify the underlined part of speech. If correct, the player places a flame on one of his candles. The first player to light all of his candles wins. Code the backs of the cards for easy self-checking.

Famous Person Gift Swap

Celebrate the holidays with favorite famous personalities. Wrap a large box and attach several cut-out tags labeled with the names of favorite book characters or historical personalities. Students choose a tag and write a story describing the gift they would give that person. Finished stories are placed inside the box for students to enjoy during their spare time.

Tom Sawyer · Zeus · Abe Lincoln · Paul Bunyan · Nero · Ramona and Beezus

Get The Travel Bug

Explore the world with real travel brochures. Mount an open questionnaire on a manila envelope, laminate, and enclose pamphlets. Update and travel anywhere by changing the questionnaire title and brochures.

• good-bye • adieu • auf Wiedersehen • vale • adios • au revoir

Travel Australia!

Use the travel brochures inside to plan your dream vacation! Decide which tour you would like to take; then answer the questions.

- How many days will you be on the tour?_____
  How many nights? _____
- What cities will you visit? _____
- What historical and/or tourist attractions will you see?
  _____
- How will the area differ geographically and climatically from
  your homeland? _____
- Why did you choose this tour? _____
- How much will the tour cost? _____
- What meals are included? _____
- From what city does your tour depart? _____
- What forms of transportation will you be using during the trip?
  _____
- Compose a letter that you might write to a friend during the last
  days of your tour. Be sure to tell what you have seen and how
  you are liking your "dream vacation."

• auf Wiedersehen • vale • adios • au revoir • au revoir

Elaine Plemons
Calhoun, GA

Helping Hands

This research project leads to a schoolwide display for Brotherhood Month in February. List names of famous people who represent many different nationalities, races, and religions. Assign students names to research. Each child writes the following information on an index card in paragraph form: name of person, country of origin, religion or race, dates of birth/death, and important contributions to the world. Students mount their cards on hands cut from colored construction paper and present their research findings to the class. Hands are displayed on doors, lockers, and walls so everyone can enjoy reading them.

Albert Einstein
Woodrow Wilson
Winston Churchill
Eleanor Roosevelt
Mahatma Gandhi
Jim Thorpe
Albert Schweitzer
Anwar el-Sadat
Andrei D. Sakharov

George Washington Carver
Martin Luther King
Marian Anderson
Jesse Jackson
Marie Curie
Eisaku Sato
Neil Armstrong
Lech Walesa
Cesar E. Chavez

Alfred Nobel
John F. Kennedy
Margaret Thatcher
Sequoyah
Helen Keller
Ralph J. Bunche
Abraham Lincoln
Menachem Begin

Booker T. Washington
Mary McLeod Bethune
Harriet Tubman
Mother Teresa
Sandra Day O'Connor
Louis Pasteur
Dag Hammarskjöld
Desmond Tutu

Jan Hodgin
High Point, NC

Give Me A Little Kiss

Give your students a "kiss" to sweeten up basic skills. Write tasks or sets of math problems on cut-out tagboard kisses. Put answers on the backs of the kisses and wrap in aluminum foil. Students unwrap a kiss and work on it in their free time. Everyone who completes the center gets a candy kiss! Make several sets of kisses and vary the skill.

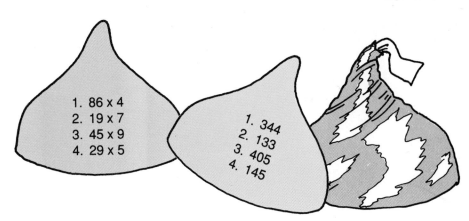

1. 86 x 4
2. 19 x 7
3. 45 x 9
4. 29 x 5

1. 344
2. 133
3. 405
4. 145

Sneaky Snakes

St. Patrick is said to have rid Ireland of all snakes. Make a St. Patrick's center full of sneaky snakes labeled with fact and opinion statements. Have students pull snake statements from St. Pat's pocket and sort the strips into fact and opinion groups.

Fact Strips

Ireland has no snakes.
Snakes are reptiles.
Most snakes hatch from eggs.
Mother snakes do not care for their babies.

No snakes eat plant food.
Snakes have many teeth.
A snake often takes four to six days to digest a meal.
Snakes hibernate in cold weather.

Opinion Strips

Snakes are ugly.
Snakes feel slimy.
All snakes should be killed.
An indigo snake is the prettiest kind of snake.

People should be afraid of snakes.
A rattlesnake is the ugliest kind of snake.
Cooked snakes taste delicious.
A snake makes a great pet.

Ann Friedman
Birmingham, AL

Spotlight on Centers

Sheet Music

Sing along with grammar practice! Type the words to a popular song and clip onto the center. Students list all the nouns, verbs, etc., they find in the song. Enlist student help in identifying new songs to use.

Anne Robinette
Centreville, MD

Grab Bag

Instead of throwing away extra math worksheets, cut them into strips so that each strip contains several problems. Drop them into a decorated "grab bag" and let children reach inside, grab a strip, and work the problems. Also great for other subject areas: vocabulary, social studies, and science review questions.

Brenda Tanner
Leesburg, VA

Safe At Home Plate!

Since students find baseball cards a popular, collectable item, create center activities to put their interest to educational uses. Suggest as many ways to use them as you can, and add more that students have created.

Here are possibilities:

- Arrange cards according to the heights of players. Tally heights. What seems to be their average height?
- Categorize the baseball team names according to the number of syllables in each.
- Using a U.S. map on a bulletin board, match cards to the cities where teams play. This may lead to a search through references.
- Make an alphabetical list of all player names.
- Use the batting records on the cards to chart players according to either home runs for the past season or the number of R.B.I.'s.
- Make a poster for each team showing its colors, emblem, and city. Laminate. Have students list the name of each player on the correct team poster. Remove marker with hairspray or nail polish remover.
- Draw state outlines for the home states of players on cards. Write player names on the appropriate state outlines.

Linda Graberti
Tulsa, OK

58

Flip Your Lid!

Large lids from margarine or dessert topping containers make easy-to-store centers. Cut two poster board circles that will fit inside the lid. Program one circle with a skill and the other with the matching answer key. Laminate and glue one to each side of the lid. Students use a wax crayon to answer the questions, then "flip their lids" to check!

Merleen Ivey
Jackson, MS

Front

Reducing Fractions Questions

1. 10/12 _____   6. 4/12 _____
2. 4/8 _____   7. 5/10 _____
3. 3/9 _____   8. 8/24 _____
4. 4/6 _____   9. 9/12 _____
5. 8/10 _____   10. 5/5 _____

Back

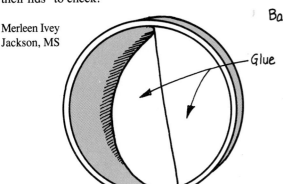

Glue

Reducing Fractions Answers

1. 5/6   6. 1/3
2. 1/2   7. 1/2
3. 1/3   8. 1/3
4. 2/3   9. 3/4
5. 4/5   10. 1/3

Album Of The Stars

All you need to make this versatile center are a magnetic photo album, some math worksheets, and your students' favorite stars! Ask students to bring in magazine and newspaper photos of famous entertainment personalities. Cut the worksheets in halves or thirds. Mount one of the minisheets with a photo on a right-hand page of the album. Add a clever caption, if desired. Place an answer key on the back of the page. A student can flip to his favorite star's page, complete the problems on his own paper, then turn the page to check his work.

BILL COSBY ANSWER KEY

1. 492   8. 332
2. 566   9. 115
3. 184   10. 189
4. 200
5. 398
6. 727
7. 113

SLY STALLONE IN "SUBTRACTION ACTION!"

1. 800	2. 400	3. 300
-198	- 79	- 72
4. 198	5. 332	6. 726
- 56	-282	-311
7. 398	8. 873	9. 593
- 98	-172	-202

Name That Capital

A Poke-and-Peek map will give a new twist to teaching state capitals. Use a transparency to enlarge a U.S. map on poster board. Laminate; then punch holes with a Kwik-Twist Paper Drill (available from The Education Center, Inc.) and label capitals on the back. Students name a city, then check by poking a pencil through a hole and looking on the back.

Eldonna Ashley
Belle Center, OH

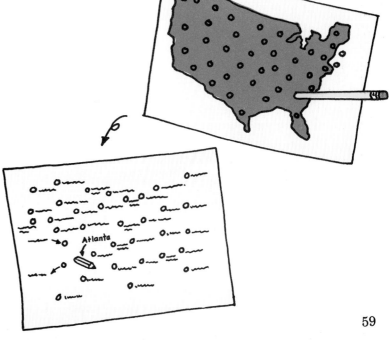

Atlanta

Countdown For The Planets

Hurry up and get on board! None of your students will want to be left behind when you blast off on a planetary tour! Prepare these activities as lesson extenders or as additions to your science learning center.

Planetary Dictionary

Have students write an ABC of the solar system that can be compiled into a *Planetary Dictionary*. Get them started by listing some words on the board; then provide colored construction paper for booklets.

A asteroids—a band of rocks which orbit between Mars and Jupiter

B Betelgeuse—star found in several constellations

C comet—mixture of ice and dust that appears to be a bright body with a tail

Blast off with a math worksheet! List problems beginning at the rocket bottom, progressing to more difficult ones at the top.

Answers:

1. 2
2. 4
3. 6
4. 20
5. 80
6. 70
7. 185
8. 73 r2
9. 125
10. 189 r2

BLAST OFF!

10. $3\overline{)569}$
9. $6\overline{)750}$
8. $4\overline{)294}$
7. $2\overline{)370}$
6. $6\overline{)420}$
5. $4\overline{)320}$
4. $2\overline{)40}$
3. $6\overline{)36}$
2. $4\overline{)16}$
1. $2\overline{)4}$

Classroom Observatory

Make your classroom look like part of the solar system! Keeping relative sizes of planets in mind, inflate balloons to different diameters and tie long strings around the knots. Then soak paper-towel strips in liquid starch and wrap around the balloons. Paint when dry and tie paper clips to the strings. Hang from the ceiling by inserting clips under ceiling panels.

Extraterrestrial Tours Unlimited

Sell an extraterrestrial tour! For a creative writing activity, future travel agents prepare brochures for the planets of their choice. They must include:

- a listing of planets on the tour

- a page of interesting facts

- items that each traveler should carry along

- time length of tour and date

- costs

- an appealing cover

Advertising Techniques

1. **The Threat:** You will be left out, ignored, or laughed at if you don't use the product.
2. **The Promise:** This car takes you on vacations, to parties, to have fun. Did you ever see an ad for a car that takes you to work?
3. **The Snob:** This product may cost you more, but you will look like a very important person.
4. **Time:** We've been in business so long our product must be good. This also seems to say that people have been buying their product a long time.
5. **Popularity:** The product is displayed in a group of happy people. This seems to say that if you use the product, you'll be in that situation also.
6. **Comfort:** Summer ads are displayed in cool settings. Winter ads are displayed in warm, snug settings. The idea is to make you think you'll be cool (or warm) if you use the product.
7. **Look At Me:** Some products show very noticeable people. The ad implies that if you use the product, people will look at you.
8. **Adventure, Excitement:** People are shown in adventurous and exciting places. If you use the product, you'll also be there, or you'll be considered adventurous and exciting.
9. **Cinderella:** Ads show some horrible example, and then a handsome or beautiful "after" shot.
10. **Pseudoscientific:** They use scientific words you can't understand, trying to impress you.

Ad Analysis

Educate young consumers about the influence of advertising. Clip ads to illustrate each ad type listed. Mount with matching captions on a bulletin board or piece of poster board. Provide several kinds of magazines, newspapers, flyers, and other promotional pieces. Students cut out five ads, glue each to a piece of paper, and label with the ad technique used. Extend by having students list the words used in the ad to influence the reader.

Mulling Over A Magazine

Capitalize on the broad appeal of magazines while you sharpen reading comprehension skills. Have students equip this center by bringing in old magazines from home. Duplicate the question sheet and store in a folder with student directions. Place the folder and magazines in a large plastic bucket or tub. Change magazines frequently for plenty of periodical practice.

Rebecca Webster Graves
Burlington, NC

1. What is the name of the magazine?
2. Who published the magazine?
3. How much does a one-year subscription cost?
4. How much is a single copy?
5. Which is the best buy?
6. Briefly describe the magazine. What type of person would find this magazine appealing?
7. Do you like the magazine? Why or why not?
8. Read an article in the magazine, and write a brief summary of what it is about.
9. Name some items or services that are advertised in the magazine.

WHAT WOULD YOU DO?

1. Take one of the cards. Read it carefully.
2. Decide what you would do if this happened to you.
3. Number your own paper. Write down what you would do first.
4. List everything you need to do to solve this problem.

What would you do if... your mom fainted

What would you do if... you lost your lunch money?

What Would You Do?

Give thinking skills a boost. These problems can be tailored to the community, classroom, or course of study. There are no correct answers. The intent of these situations is to develop sequences in the problem-solving process. Change the problems each week.

What Would You Do If

1. ...you were lost in the forest?
2. ...you were a pioneer child on a wagon train to California?
3. ...a pan of grease on the stove caught fire?
4. ...you lost your lunch money?
5. ...your house was on fire?
6. ...your mom fainted?
7. ...you came home and you thought a burglar had been in your house?
8. ...you had one week to earn $50.00 for a trip to Disney World?

Star Search

Create multipurpose task cards with the help of today's popular stars. Have students bring in copies of their favorite teen magazines. Cut out short articles, mount on tagboard, and laminate. Use the articles for a variety of skills. Students can write original comprehension questions about each article for classmates to answer. Have students outline the articles or identify the topic sentence of each paragraph. Give each student a card and have him write a friendly or business letter to the star. For math practice, have students write word problems based on the articles' information.

Math Circle

For a reusable math center, cut out a large poster board circle. Divide into numbered sections as shown; then laminate. Using a wipe-off marker, write directions in the center circle and numbers in the sections around it. Place open worksheets as shown at the center. The student takes a worksheet, solves the problems on the back, and writes his answers in the numbered sections. To use the center again, wipe it clean and add new directions and numbers.

Ann Runyon
Littleton, CO

Who "Dunnit"?

Spin the wheels to find out WHAT was stolen, WHERE it was stolen from, and WHEN it was taken. Use this information to write a paragraph—you supply WHO is guilty and WHY!!!

WHAT? 50 million dollars

WHEN? Sept. 23, 1980

WHERE? Pittsburgh National Bank

(wheel words: diamonds, a famous painting, all of the food, everyone's clothes, the President's car)

(wheel words: the library, Ben Franklin Elementary School, NBC Studios, Europe, Spooky Castle)

(wheel words: yesterday, on your birthday, 100 years ago, in the middle of the night)

← back →

Who "Dunnit"?

Let your creative students help you think of some words and phrases to write on the poster board wheels!

Arlene D. Novels
Indiana, PA

Album Centers

Turn magnetic photo albums into learning centers! Mount worksheets, workbook pages, and activity cards in the books. Students take albums to their desks and work with wipe-off crayons. Place answer keys at the back of each book for self-checking.

Gail Hutchinson
Beverly, MA

What's The Angle?

Practice with a protractor makes geometry come alive for intermediate students. Cut out and label several angle figures and place in an envelope. Prepare task cards asking questions about the angles. Students select a card and use a protractor to answer the questions. Place a coded answer key for each task card inside the envelope.

Task Card A
1. How many degrees is angle C?
2. How many degrees is angle A?
3. Can you make an angle 10° larger than angle G?

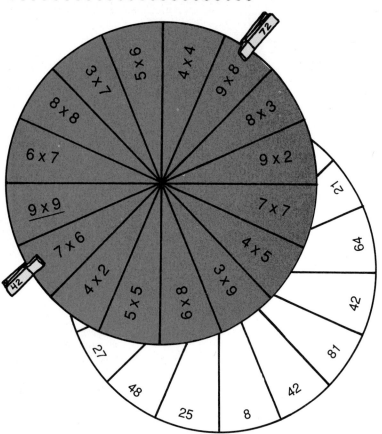

Pizza Math

Let pizza wheels add flavor to your classroom. The possibilities for use in math seem endless. Nell Gardner Warrenton, NC, sends us the following examples:

wheel	clothespin
△	triangle
67	sixty-seven
9 x 4	36
%	percent
◑	1/4
500 + 20 +6	526
XI	11
2/4	1/2
3/2	1 1/2
1, 3, 5,_____	7
25%	1/4
∠→	acute angle
∠	45°
kilo-	1,000

On The Road

Get summer rolling with a map-reading center! Laminate and post a road map. Provide task cards for students to complete. Mark specific areas on the map with a wipe-off crayon or with tacks and yarn.

- What highway connects Atlanta and Augusta, GA?
- How many cities are within 20 miles of Knoxville, TN?
- If you travel 40 miles north of Jacksonville, FL, on Highway 95, what city will you reach?
- How far is it from Jackson, MS, to Memphis, TN (using Highway 55)?

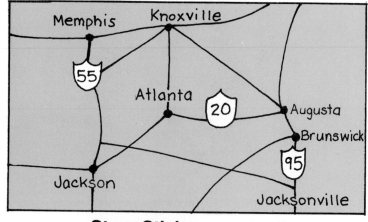

Story Sticks

Your students will love chewing on these funny story starters. To make the center, fold a piece of poster board in half. Staple as shown to make a giant gum wrapper. Write story starters on white poster board strips. Store the "story sticks" inside the wrapper. Reward students who complete a story with a piece of sugarless bubble gum—YUM!

Sample story starters:
- Life as a piece of gum, stuck on the bottom of someone's shoe, isn't easy! Today I ...
- My recipe for a new bubble gum flavor was finished! But when I began mixing the ingredients ...
- My first day as the manager of a bubble gum factory was terrible! First, ...
- When I opened the pack of gum, there was a message inside. I read the message and ...
- If I were a piece of pineapple bubble gum, I would ...

Do all of the tasks below:

1. Choose a foreign country. Mark it in color on an outline map.
2. Make a chart showing temperature range and rainfall.
3. Cut out pictures of the country, or draw an outstanding feature.
4. Write a report of at least five paragraphs telling the capital, population, type of government, currency, geographic features, and products.
5. Write a story about a child of your chosen country. Tell about his home, food, clothing, and favorite activities.

Choose two of the following:

1. Invite a person from your chosen country to speak to the class.
2. Write to a foreign pen pal, and share your letters with the class.
3. Make a foreign food to share with the class.
4. Ask a travel agent for brochures or posters to display.
5. Draw a map of your chosen country. Label important cities, geographic features, and products.
6. Act out an interview with a foreign friend. One person can be the news reporter and the other the foreign child. Ask questions about his food, clothing, school, and play.
7. Learn to say something in the foreign language.

Children Around The World

While studying other countries of the world, have students gather information for a "Children Around The World" notebook. Display maps of the different areas of the world. Provide outline maps for students to color in their appropriate areas. Also provide resource materials at the center.

Students choose a country or area to study individually or in a group. At the center, provide a contract of basic tasks to be completed. As students complete assignments, have them add pages to a "Children Around The World" class notebook.

Kathy Beard
Keystone Heights, FL

Geometric Symbol Math

Looking for an easy morning math activity? Use the worksheet on page 66 all year long to drill addition of whole numbers, decimals, or fractions. Duplicate a copy of the sheet for each student. Draw the five shapes on the board and fill in with numbers. Students write the numbers in the matching shapes on their worksheets, then add. The next time you want to use the sheet, duplicate more copies, draw shapes again on the board, and fill in with different numbers.

Jeanne Mullineaux
Unadilla, NY

Geometric Symbol Math

Fill in the shapes with the numbers on the board.
Work the problem to find the sum.

EXAMPLE

365   558   558

365
558
+ 558

1,481

Best of THE MAILBOX • INTERMEDIATE • ©The Education Center, Inc. • Jeanne Mullineaux, Unadilla, NY

66   **Note To Teacher:** See directions for using this sheet on page 65.

Celebrate UNITED NATIONS DAY

Students should appreciate the complexity of maintaining international cooperation among world nations after participating in this United Nations Day simulation. The activity involves the whole class and is both challenging and fun.

Debbie Wiggins
Myrtle Beach, SC

Background

The United Nations was established on October 24, 1945. Its purpose is to cooperate in solving international problems, while promoting peace, freedom, and equality. In 1985, 159 nations belonged to the United Nations. Politics and the emergence of new nations cause the membership to fluctuate. Members meet at the organization's headquarters in New York City to discuss world problems. The United Nations has several branches. One of its branches, the United Nations Children's Fund (UNICEF), was created in 1946 to provide clothing, blankets, and medicine to children who needed help after World War II. The organization has continued to serve the needs of children all over the world. On Halloween, many children "trick-or-treat" for UNICEF. Selling greeting cards is another popular way UNICEF raises money.

Preparation

Begin a few days prior to United Nations Day (October 24). Check a current World Almanac for a list of member nations.

Each student picks a country to represent on United Nations Day. He researches the problems, flag, geography, and dress of the country and writes a report. The student draws a map of the country and its national flag.

Presentation

On United Nations Day, arrange desks in a circle. Students tape their countries' names and flags to the fronts of their desks. Students dress in the style of the country. Each student introduces himself, then summarizes the problems and concerns of his country.

As chairman, the teacher announces a crisis and requests help from the council in solving it. (Example: OPEC countries are unable to supply the world with oil because of a freak storm that has destroyed their ships.) Student delegates discuss the problem and possible solutions. New treaties or pacts are made, if needed, to solve the problem.

Library Book Team

Encourage children to read books through this friendly battle of minds. The "Battle of the Books" was a citywide competition in Greensboro, NC, sponsored by the public library. It may be adapted to a school- or districtwide tournament. The objective is for student teams to answer questions about books by stating titles and authors. Questions may be submitted by students, teachers, or librarians during the year and are filed on 3" × 5" cards.

Choose equal numbers of easy and difficult questions from several categories for each team, and match in pairs. Follow easy questions with difficult ones. Organize questions with several easy ones at the beginning of a contest to build confidence. For grades 4–6, about 20 questions are standard.

To play, divide students into groups of three to five, or match half the class against the other half. Choose a scorekeeper, a timekeeper, and an announcer. Provide a score sheet. Play contest as indicated in the rules. Provide prizes such as paperbacks, gift certificates from bookstores, or trophies to winning tournament teams. A special prize to each participant is an extra motivator.

Sandra Neerman
Elizabeth Buie
Chartee Plyler
Hope Gooch
Cynthia Brown

Greensboro Public Library, Greensboro, NC
Idea from "Battle of the Books—Urbana Style" by Joanne Kelly
School Library Journal

Rules For The Battle:

1. Players are divided into teams of equal numbers.
2. Each team will be asked an equal number of questions. Questions are addressed to the teams alternately, regardless of which team last gave a correct answer. Team One will therefore receive all odd-numbered questions and Team Two all even-numbered ones.
3. Five points are scored by a team giving the correct title of a book. After a team has given the title, it may score three additional points by correctly identifying the author of the book.
4. The team to which a question is addressed has 30 seconds in which to give both the title and the author of the book. During that time team members have as many guesses as they wish and anyone on the team may try.
5. If at the end of 30 seconds a team is unable to answer a question correctly, the opposing team is allowed the chance to give the title and author immediately.

Sample Questions For Battle Of The Books:

1. In what book was a young boy killed by a pack of wild dogs?
2. In what book does a mouse save Jeremy the crow after he becomes tangled up in a piece of string?
3. In what book was a cricket accused of causing a fire in the newsstand?
4. In what book is there a monkey named Mr. Nillson?
5. In which book did a girl give her friend a box of watercolor paints, brushes, and art paper, which he later threw away?
6. In what book does a first-grader have a chance to tell about her new bedroom for Show-and-Tell?
7. In which book is William given a plaid sport jacket to help him return home?
8. In what book did a young girl become a "Crusader" for the rights of her new neighbors?
9. In what books does a very young detective solve cases for 25¢ a day?
10. In what book are Willie the Fieldmouse, Phewie the Skunk, and Uncle Analdas some of the main characters?
11. In what book were three kisses very important?
12. In what book do a little girl and her dog fall asleep in a field of bright red flowers?

Island Of The Blue Dolphins, Scott O'Dell (1)
Mrs. Frisby And The Rats Of NIMH, Robert C. O'Brien (2)
Cricket In Times Square, George Selden (3)
Pippi Longstocking, Astrid Lindgren (4)
Bridge To Terabithia, Katherine Paterson (5)
Ramona The Brave, Beverly Cleary (6)

Fat Men From Space, Daniel Pinkwater (7)
Iggie's House, Judy Blume (8)
Encyclopedia Brown books, Donald Sobol (9)
Rabbit Hill, Robert Lawson (10)
Strega Nona, Tomie de Paola (11)
Wizard Of Oz, L. Frank Baum (12)

Going Once, Going Twice, Sold!

Famous People Auction

JUNE 7TH   *JUNE 7TH*

Photographs • Pennants • Baseballs • Baseball Cards • Soccer Balls
Medallions • Books • Albums • Toys • Games • Coins • Stamps

Diane Murray, a reading teacher in Troy, Michigan, has found a way to beat the reading blues! Her second- through fifth-grade students at Hill Elementary School are planning to bid on celebrity-donated items at a "Famous People Auction." Students will be spending play money they've earned by reading books, accumulating one "penny" per page. Now readers who were once reluctant are eagerly reading for a chance to own some very special momentos.

The plans got under way last October when Ms. Murray wrote to entertainers, politicians, and prominent business leaders, asking them to contribute items students would like to buy at auction. The response was wonderful. Thanks to President Reagan, Detroit Lions kicker Ed Murray, the "Dallas" cast, and the late University of Alabama football coach Paul "Bear" Bryant, there will be autographed photographs up for bid. Other items to be treasured include a medallion donated by Frank Borman, a former astronaut. The medal traveled aboard *Apollo 8* on a trip to the moon. Parents are donating additional gifts for the big event.

Many students have already chosen items they'll bid on in the June 7th auction, and they'll tell you that Ms. Murray's idea has gotten them more excited about reading than ever before!

If you're looking for a fresh, new approach that makes reading a positive experience, hold a readers' auction. Enlist parent help as Ms. Murray did, include student-made crafts, or perhaps contributions from co-teachers. As with the eager readers at Hill Elementary, it's sure to be a big hit with your students!

The Great Debate

Can you name the future debaters in your class? They're the ones who can argue with a fencepost and win! Why not channel these abilities into guided debates, and in the process develop the skills of assembling, organizing, interpreting, and presenting information clearly and concisely?

Getting Ready

The key to a strong debate is in being well armed. This does not mean you have to do a lot of work in gathering information. Let students do the research while you guide their efforts.

- Have the class watch a morning news program each day. After each segment, discuss key events and topics that students have questions or strong feelings about.

- If you don't have access to a classroom TV, designate committees to present daily reports after watching the TV or listening to a radio at home.

- After a week of examining current world events, students can compose questions for a quiz to check their facts and understanding.

- At this point, students should be able to help you list topics on the board that would lend themselves to a debate.

The Debate

Introduce the format by holding a mock debate with the entire class.

1. Decide on a proposal from your list of topics.

2. Have two teams with the same number of members take opposite sides of the proposal.

3. Members must research the proposal and list as much evidence as they can that would prove it true or false. Facts or opinions may be used. Members should list just as much about the opposing standpoint as their own.

4. In turn, each side presents an issue, or evidence, and is answered by the opposing team, until all issues have been discussed.

5. Designate student judges to give points to the team that wins each issue.

After a practice run, divide students into small evenly numbered groups, allowing "extras" to serve as judges. Let them select their proposals, and they're on their own to develop and present great debates!

Topics For Starters

1. Use of pocket calculators in the classroom.
2. The U.S. involvement in nuclear weapon control.
3. Methods of protecting endangered species.
4. Alternatives to overcrowding in prisons.
5. Keeping schools in session all year.
6. Industries' responsibilities in pollution control.
7. Classroom use of comic books.

Brainstormers

Encourage students to express limitless ideas in a small group situation. Divide the class into small groups, and let each group choose a recording secretary. Supply groups with paper and a pencil. Explain the brainstormer activity as a thinking activity in which any and all ideas are accepted, the more the better. Students should strive for as many ideas as possible. Set a time limit. Give the category, and turn groups loose. When the time is up, have each secretary read the group's list with the class deleting answers that don't qualify. The group with the longest list wins!

Activity 1 . . . Reality
Assign groups to make a list of as many as possible:

vegetables	musical instruments	stores
holidays	things to wear on your feet	color words
things used to write	four-syllable words	careers
tree varieties	countries	dog breeds
automobile models	soda pops	cereals
famous athletes	flower varieties	Easter symbols
things that fly	movies	things that roll
things to buy for under $1.00	famous women	

Activity 2 . . . Imagination/Originality
Assign groups to list . . .

uses for last year's calendar	new subjects to take in school
new themes for amusement parks	ways to travel
new color words	uses for a lemon
contests to enter	places to go on vacation
uses for an ice cube	things to wear on your head
new holidays	new foods
uses for paper clips	things that should be invented

Activity 3 . . . Situations
Explain a situation to the groups. They are to decide on as many solutions as possible. To vary, assign them to give only ridiculous, sensible, or poor solutions.

You found a wallet containing three $100 bills on the sidewalk.
Someone delivered 75 crates of ripe tomatoes to your house.
You looked in the mirror one morning and saw that your face was green.
Someone left a basket of 23 kittens on your doorstep.
You looked out the window and saw a dinosaur.
Due to bad weather, the Easter rabbit asked you to help deliver eggs.

Mary Jo Bailin
Toledo, OH

A Time For Trees

Arbor Day, first proposed in 1872 by Julius Sterling Morton, is a day meant for the planting of trees. Most often honored by schoolchildren, the day lends itself to a variety of activities. The date of celebration in your area may differ because of the differences in planting seasons.

Rebecca Webster Graves of Burlington, North Carolina, suggests several Arbor Day activities that emphasize the interdependence of man and nature. The ideas can be used as individual, small group, or class projects. Label two identical construction paper leaves for each activity and post on a bulletin board. Students remove the top leaf for instructions and sign the remaining leaf. This serves as a contract to be dated when the activity is completed. Have students display and explain their projects when finished.

Kick off your Arbor Day celebration by sharing tree-inspired literature including the Johnny Appleseed legend, Joyce Kilmer's "Trees," and *The Giving Tree* by Shel Silverstein.

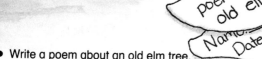

Write a poem about an old elm tree.

Name: _____ Date: _____

- Write a poem about an old elm tree.
- Take a walking tour of the school grounds. List the kinds of trees you see. Then list trees as deciduous or evergreen.
- Write a song about a pine tree and teach it to the class.
- Make a poster showing the ways you can help a tree grow.
- Research and report on Julius Sterling Morton and his involvement with Arbor Day.
- Cut photographs from magazines showing industrial use of lumber. Paste on poster board and label.
- Make a papier-mâché model of a palm tree. Label the parts.
- Write and present a play that explains how forests provide homes for animals.
- Investigate and report on the causes of erosion and its effects on trees. How can erosion be prevented?
- Take a walk in the woods to discover birds, animals, or insects that depend on trees in your area. Chart your findings.
- Bring a cross section of a trunk or limb to class. Label the outer and inner bark, cambium, annual rings, sapwood, and heartwood.
- Plant a fruit tree seed and keep a record of its development.
- Try to list everything in the classroom that comes from trees. Put your list in alphabetical order.
- Make a poster showing the root system of a tree. Label and explain the purposes of the different types.
- Make a list of the official state trees.
- Make a leaf collection, including seeds of the trees.
- Find out the mature heights of ten different trees. Record the information in a picture graph.
- Write your state forester to find out what some enemies of trees are. How are they controlled?
- Research the practices being used in the selection of timber for cutting.
- Conduct interviews of ten classmates to discover what their favorite trees are and why. Report the results to your class.

Irene M. Wakeham

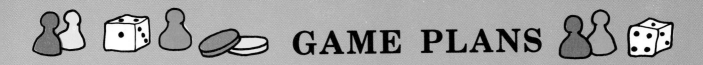

GAME PLANS

Tic-Tac-School

Draw and label a grid as shown on the chalkboard. Prepare several question cards for each category. Divide the class into teams *X* and *O*. In turn, teams select categories, answer questions, and claim squares when correct. First with three in a row wins!

Note: This game may be used all year by providing new cards and saving the old cards for next year.

Shirley Moore
Rapid City, SD

① Reading	② Math	③ Odds and Ends
④ Language	⑤ Math Story Problems	⑥ Social Studies
⑦ Spelling	⑧ Health	⑨ Science

Spelling Shoeboxes

Provide each row in your class with a shoebox containing a set of alphabet cards. (Be sure each set has three to four cards of each letter.) Call out a word. The first person in the row finds the first letter of the word, then passes the box to the second person, who finds the second letter, and so on. The first row to correctly spell the word wins. Easy to store and pull out to play any day.

Lynn Martin
Blanchester, OH

Reduce-a-Fraction
2–4 players

Prepare a wheel with a spinner and playing cards to show the fractions on the chart. Deal cards among players. Each student spins. If a player can reduce the fraction on one of his cards to the fraction spun, he discards that card. First player to discard all cards wins.

Hattie Turner
Bassett, VA

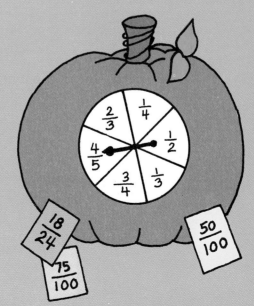

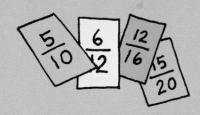

CARDS

$\frac{1}{4}$ =	$\frac{2}{8}$	$\frac{3}{12}$	$\frac{4}{16}$	$\frac{5}{20}$	$\frac{6}{24}$	$\frac{25}{100}$	
$\frac{1}{3}$ =	$\frac{2}{6}$	$\frac{3}{9}$	$\frac{4}{12}$	$\frac{5}{15}$	$\frac{6}{18}$	$\frac{25}{75}$	
$\frac{2}{3}$ =	$\frac{4}{6}$	$\frac{6}{9}$	$\frac{8}{12}$	$\frac{10}{15}$	$\frac{12}{18}$	$\frac{50}{75}$	
$\frac{3}{4}$ =	$\frac{6}{8}$	$\frac{9}{12}$	$\frac{12}{16}$	$\frac{15}{20}$	$\frac{18}{24}$	$\frac{75}{100}$	
$\frac{4}{5}$ =	$\frac{8}{10}$	$\frac{12}{15}$	$\frac{16}{20}$	$\frac{20}{25}$	$\frac{24}{30}$	$\frac{80}{100}$	
$\frac{1}{2}$ =	$\frac{2}{4}$	$\frac{3}{6}$	$\frac{4}{8}$	$\frac{5}{10}$	$\frac{6}{12}$	$\frac{50}{100}$	

Musical Math

Students get on the move with a musical math review. Place a math problem card on each desk and begin a popular record. Students copy and solve the problem. When the music stops, everyone moves to the next desk and follows the same procedure. Continue until students have worked their way around the room and back to their own desks.

Janet Boyd
Chandler, OK

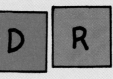

Vocabulary Dig-It!

Students will dig into vocabulary and spelling practice with this fast-paced game. Two to ten players can play. Obtain printed alphabet letter cards, which are packaged in quantity, and dump them in the center of a table. Make a deck of 80 subject cards. Shuffle and deal five subject cards, facedown, to each player.

At a signal, all players turn their top cards over. Each digs into the pile of letters to spell a word that describes his subject. Only one letter may be picked up at a time. Each player places the spelled word beside his subject card, then turns over his next subject. The first person to complete all five subjects calls, "Stop digging!" All digging stops at once, and the caller reads his cards and spelled words.

If all are correct, the winner receives points equal to the number of unanswered subject cards his opponents have left. If incorrect, he gives his opponents two points each. After all points are paid, the deal passes to the left for the next round. To vary, play with decks for synonyms and antonyms.

Nancy F. Harvey
Webster, TX

Pickle Race

Students make a mad dash for reference books when running the Pickle Race. Set out five or more reference sources: the atlas, almanac, dictionary, encyclopedia, and thesaurus. Write questions on green, paper pickles and place them in a clear jar. Each day, students write answers to questions on slips of paper. Have students keep a record of questions they have completed on a wall chart, and keep a duplicate record of students' answers in your grade book. Set a limit for the number of questions students answer each day. At the end of the "race," reward students who have answered a prearranged number correctly.

Janis Ludwig
Battle Creek, MI

Sample Questions:
What is the capital of the United States?
How many stomachs does a cow have?
Who is buried in Grant's Tomb?
What is the record for the largest banana split?
How many people attended the world's largest funeral?
What would you do with a *rutabaga?*

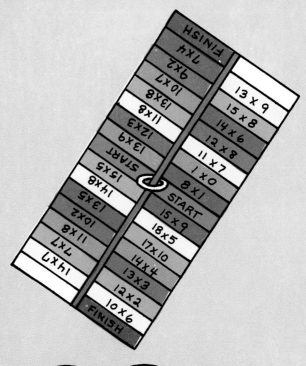

Tug-of-War

Two players compete in this math tug-of-war game. A rubber band [p]iece of yarn with a washer attached is stretched end to end around the [gam]eboard. The washer serves as a common marker. Each player selects [a] side of the gameboard. In turn, players roll a die, move the washer [tow]ards their finish line, and answer the problem. If incorrect, the [play]er loses a turn. First to reach a finish line wins.

[.] Marshall Sperry
[Dec]atur, IL

7-Up Shake-up

Children will love a new twist to this old favorite! Upon "heads down," all students put their heads down with eyes closed. Seven players walk quietly around the room and tap one class member each. As a student is tapped, he raises his hand. When the seven players have selected seven others, they return to the front, hold up state name cards, and call out, "Seven Up!" The class members selected stand and try to guess who picked them. They must call out the capitals of the states shown instead of the players' names. If they guess the correct person and give the correct capital, they take the original player's place and game resumes. Vary with continent outlines, state abbreviations, etc.

Gayle Etter
Vermilion, OH

Word Chains

Word Chains is a challenging game for practicing parts of speech. Best of all, it requires no extra materials. To start a word chain, the teacher calls out a part of speech to be used, such as, "noun," and an example, such as, "elephant." The first student must give another noun beginning with the last letter of the word just given (*t*). The chain continues until all students have had a chance to reply. To increase the difficulty, ask for "green nouns," "huge nouns," or "nouns that breathe"! Great for other parts of speech, too!

Language Tic-Tac-Toe

[ ] Play tic-tac-toe with your class to review parts of speech. [Ea]ch student draws a grid on a sheet of paper and numbers [th]e squares randomly from 1 to 9. (Make sure that the [nu]mbers are small and in the corner of each box.) Call out a [nu]mber and a word. Children write "*N*" in the numbered [sq]uare if the word is a noun, "*V*" if it is a verb. Winners [ha]ve three *N's* or three *V's* in a row. Vary using subject/ [pr]edicate sentence parts, long-/short-vowel words, or [tru]e/false statements.

[n]a Palmer
[Wo]lcott, CT

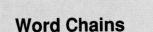

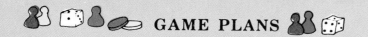
Challengers Question Game

Encourage careful reading with some classroom competition. Divide the class into two teams. Have them read an article silently, to each other, or in small groups. Students ask the other team important questions about the article. As a team, players decide on the correct answer to each question and have a spokesman give the answer. Each correct answer is worth one point. An incorrect answer gives the opposing team a chance for an extra point. Teams try to stump each other with well-chosen questions. Use this for a quick review of science, social studies, or health facts.

Pattern Picks

Take the blahs out of oral reading drill. Have students guess the pattern you are using to choose children to read! Call on students wearing layers of clothing, those wearing green, ones sitting in "odd" seats, and students who have blue eyes. Once your students get the hang of the game, have them suggest new patterns.

Joyce Hodge
Orange Park, FL

Ghost

Foster spelling and vocabulary growth with this simplified version of "Ghost." To play, ask one child to write any letter on the chalkboard. The next child goes to the board and writes a second letter, taking care not to finish the word. Any student who finishes a word drops out of the game. When that happens, the next child starts a new word. Play continues until every child has had a turn.

Isobel L. Livingstone
Rahway, NJ

Circle Math Relay

Build accuracy and speed for multiplication practice. Divide the class into teams. Draw a large circle on the board for each team. Draw a smaller circle in the center of each large one. Write numbers around the inside edge of each big circle as shown.

The first player on each team stands in front of his circle. Call out a number. Players write the number in the smaller circle and multiply it by each number on the larger circle. The products are put on the outside of the large circle. The first player to finish with all correct answers gets two points for his team. Players on the other teams who complete the problems and have all correct answers get one point for their teams. The next team members go to the board and erase the center number and products outside the large circle. Call out a new number. Continue to play until everyone has had a turn. The team with the most points wins.

The Pinballs—
A Read-aloud Favorite

With wit and poignancy, author Betsy Byars chronicles the disappointment and determination of three foster children who feel as unsettled as pinballs. The easy-to-read dialogue and short chapters will make *The Pinballs* a favorite among students. Follow up reading with these creative activities.

Pinball Pictures

The Pinballs—Carlie, Harvey, and Thomas J—are three different children with similar problems. As a class, list adjectives on the board to describe each of the Pinballs. Then have each student use one of the lists to write a character sketch of Carlie, Harvey, or Thomas J.

After the sketches are written, have each child cover a large tagboard circle with aluminum foil to make a pinball. The student copies his character sketch on a smaller circle of notebook paper which he then glues on his pinball. Post the pinballs on a bulletin board. Let students create other pinballs illustrated with favorite scenes from the book.

Harvey's Lists

One of the ways Harvey coped with being a foster child was to make lists in his special notebook: Bad Things That Have Happened To Me, Books That I Have Enjoyed, Gifts I Got That I Didn't Want. Encourage your students to become list-makers. As a class, brainstorm titles of unusual lists like Harvey's. Have a student volunteer make a copy of the list of titles for you. When you have a few extra minutes, write one of the titles on the board. Challenge students to list as many items as possible in three to five minutes.

If You Could Talk To The Pinballs

Get your students thinking about Betsy Byars's character development with an interesting writing assignment. After reading the first six chapters of *The Pinballs,* discuss with students what they have learned about the mannerisms, personality, and manner of speaking of each of the three children. Then have each student write a conversation between himself and one of the Pinballs. Share finished conversations; then file the papers away.

At the conclusion of the book, discuss how each character has changed. How would a conversation with him or her be different from the first? Have each student write another conversation with his character and compare it with the earlier conversation.

Fifteen Minutes Of Fame

In *The Pinballs,* Harvey reads that one day everybody will be famous for 15 minutes. Ask your students how they would complete this sentence: "If I could be famous for 15 minutes, I would..." Have each student illustrate his reply on a class mural. Post the mural in a hallway with the title "Fantasies Of Fame."

Rabbit Hill

Little Georgie and the Animals spend days anxiously waiting for their new neighbors. What kind of people will they be? The New Folks who arrive are indeed kind and care a great deal about their Rabbit Hill friends. Extend the pleasure of reading Robert Lawson's *Rabbit Hill* with these activities and the related worksheet on page 80.

Howdy, Neighbors!

The occupants of Rabbit Hill waited for the New Folks' arrival with great anticipation. Would they be gentle, planting Folks or shiftless like the last ones? Discuss students' feelings toward new neighbors, before and after meeting them. Decide on ways of welcoming someone to a community. Then vote on a classroom "welcome wagon" committee to make new students feel at home. Committee members can prepare a basket filled with "welcome" surprises for the new students:

- school handbook
- coupon good for a tour of the school with a committee member
- minibag of school supplies
- class list of student names
- stickers or bookmarks
- copy of the school newspaper

Sylvia J. Foust
Long Beach, NC

Proud To Be Me

Georgie felt great pride when he jumped Deadman's Brook in a single bound. Focus on improving self-concept by making a class "Proud to Be Me" booklet. Have each student write a paragraph describing a personal achievement of which he is particularly proud. After adding illustrations, compile a class book. For an added touch of fun, have students decorate cut-out T-shirts with nicknames such as Georgie did when he referred to himself as "Georgie the Leaper."

A Case Of The Worries

Mother was quite a worrier—particularly about her family and Little Georgie. After discussing reasons why people worry, have students suggest "prescriptions" to cure someone of "the worries." Children can write their prescriptions on construction paper pill bottles and post them on a bulletin board titled, "RX for the Worries."

Food For Thought

Should wild animals be fed by humans or not? Discuss the consequences of feeding bears, chipmunks, squirrels, or other wild animals. Have students list pros and cons on the subject, then take their lists home for parents' contributions. Follow up with a class discussion on effects either approach would have on the normal ecological balance. Invite a park ranger or naturalist to speak to your students. Conclude by having students make posters which give their opinions on the subject.

Senior Slogans

Elderly Uncle Analdas was highly respected for his knowledge of the countryside and escape techniques. Follow up a discussion of how we benefit from the experience of older relatives and friends with a slogan-writing session. Write phrases on pennant cutouts and post for an Open House display.

Cards For Critters

The New Folks rescued Little Georgie from his highway accident. If he had been ignored, he probably would have died. Encourage students to share experiences involving wounded animals. Use this as an opportunity to stress that handling wild animals is not recommended. Just for fun, have students design get-well cards, including jingles, with a sick animal in mind.

Moving Day Predictions

When the moving vans were unloaded, the animals eagerly watched, making predictions about the New Folks. Encourage thinking skills with this group activity. Label approximately 30 cards with unusual items. Divide the class into groups and give each group five cards. Have groups pretend that the items on their cards have just been unloaded from their new neighbors' moving van. What do the items indicate about their neighbors' character, hobbies, and family? Have groups list their items and predictions on large cut-out vans to share with the other groups.

Items	Predictions
Ice skates	They are interested in science and art.
Telescope	Maybe one of the parents is an
3 beat-up bicycles	astronomer. They may have children
An artist's easel	who are grown since the bikes are old.
Large bag of birdseed	They may have birds as pets.

Dear Mr. McGrath

At the end of the book, the garden is undisturbed and Tim McGrath, the gardener, is bewildered. The New Folks didn't use a fence, traps, or poison to keep animals out. Have students choose an animal character and write a letter to Tim to explain why the animals left the New Folks' garden alone. Writers should keep their animals' personality traits in mind to make the letters sound authentic.

Crossword Creations

Take advantage of Father's eloquent vocabulary! Provide graph paper and dictionaries; then challenge students to incorporate these words in homemade crossword puzzles:

invaluable	auspicious
flippant	indulgence
ascertain	ménage
felicitous	negligible
propitious	perilous
renaissance	render
provender	acute
indubitably	beneficial

Rabbit Habits

For each underlined word, circle the letter in the correct column.
Write the circled letters in the numbered blanks below.

	NOUN	VERB	ADVERB	ADJECTIVE
1. The female rabbit is called the doe, and the male is called the <u>buck</u>.	O	J	C	E
2. A nest of <u>dry</u> grass is lined with down from the doe's body.	L	O	M	R
3. A <u>newborn</u> rabbit is hairless and blind.	I	B	K	A
4. Rabbits <u>signal</u> to each other by displaying their white tails.	T	F	N	T
5. They <u>prefer</u> to go out at night and sleep during the day.	J	P	S	A
6. Rabbits defend themselves by keeping still or by running <u>away</u>.	C	G	W	E
7. They can run up to <u>forty</u> miles an hour.	I	L	H	O
8. They change directions <u>quickly</u> to confuse the enemy.	N	Q	E	F
9. In autumn, rabbits eat more to prepare for winter's slim food <u>supply</u>.	R	K	P	M
10. The rabbit's senses of smell and hearing are <u>very</u> sharp.	D	J	T	O

A rabbit's fur is tightly packed, which helps make it

___ ___ ___ ___ ___ ___ ___ ___ ___ ___ .
  6   3   10   8   2   5   9   1   7   4

There are two main types of wild rabbits, *cottontails* and *European rabbits*.
Domestic rabbits are tame varieties of European rabbits.
On the back of this sheet, write each list of rabbits in alphabetical order.

Cottontails: mountain cottontail, New England cottontail, desert cottontail, eastern cottontail
Domestic Rabbits: Californian, New Zealand, Chinchilla, Angora, Florida White, Belgian hare, Netherland Dwarf, White Flemish Giant, Palomino, Havana, Rex

Bonus Box: Rabbit fur has been replaced by artificial furs in most clothing. But Angora rabbits are still raised for their long, white fur. The hairs are plucked from the animals' coats and spun into soft, warm yarn for sweaters and other clothing. Do you think it is right to still use real rabbit fur in clothing? Write your opinion.

A Wrinkle In Time

This Newbery Award winner is a magical tale by Madeleine L'Engle. The story centers on a missing father, his youngest son who has a unique essence, and three inspiring heavenly travelers. Magic that could easily seem real is created by space travel via the *tesseract* and the Murry family experiments in science and math. Is this story science fiction or a premonition of our real scientific future? Enjoy the story and these accompanying activities, plus the worksheet on page 83.

Protectors Of The Universe

Mrs. Whatsit, Mrs. Who, and Mrs. Which are central characters never fully explained by the author. They are compared to supernatural beings, to witches, and to guardian angels. It is up to the reader to define them. So old that they're ageless, and known throughout the universe, they are indeed powerful. The three are on a mission to help find Mr. Murry.

Pretend that you have supernatural powers for helping others less fortunate. Define one of your assignments and describe your adventures. Portray this by a skit, a tape, a story, a picture story in multiple frames, or another project.

The Tesseract, The Only Way To Travel

The tesseract/tessering is a form of travel in the story. Mr. and Mrs. Murry, both scientists, experimented with it. Whatsit, Which, and Who used it proficiently. Related to the fifth dimension, it incorporates size, volume, time, and something more. Travel through space is therefore possible "without going the long way around." Another name for tessering is *wrinkling*.

Science fiction movies, stories, and TV programs often employ a version of tessering, such as "beaming a character up or down" on "Star Trek." Write about a version that you've seen or read about. Make up a form of this travel for yourself. Describe it in detail, including advantages, sensations, danger, etc. Do you believe that it may someday happen?

First, Second, And Third Dimensions

To understand tessering, it is necessary to grasp the three dimensions forming art and visual awareness. The first takes space but has no area, the second has area, and the third has volume.

Illustrate examples of each in either a sequential picture or in a separate picture for each dimension. Draw or cut and glue pictures from magazines, catalogs, math textbooks, etc.

The Black Thing

Traveling through the universe, the characters *tessered* through The Black Thing and saw its evil shadow surrounding planets. The Black Thing is the Powers of Darkness.

Some of the very best fighters against it have come from Earth. They include Jesus, da Vinci, Michelangelo, Shakespeare, Bach, Pasteur, Madame Curie, Gandhi, Buddha, Rembrandt, and others.

Join the battle against The Black Thing. Write, draw, or demonstrate how you will fight it and what you're fighting.

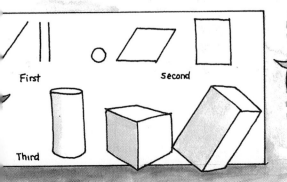

First

Second

Third

Take A Closer Look

Whatsit, Which, and Who teach three children to go beyond their limited visual perception of reality. They enlighten the youngsters to the notion that things may not indeed be as they first appeared.

Have students list characteristics of Whatsit, Which, and Who in three columns on their paper. Here's a list for you:

Whatsit	Which	Who
awkward lady	booming voice	plump, little woman
several, assorted	black robe	enormous spectacles
colored scarves	black, peaked hat	quick with needle
man's felt hat	beady eyes	and thread
rough overcoat	beaked nose	recites famous quotes
black, rubber boots	one bony claw	in all languages
	holding broomstick	

Consider reasons for their different appearances. If you had their powers and could choose your appearance at will, write about and illustrate your choice. Indicate changes occurring due to age, situation, or environment.

Something Special About Them

Charles Wallace and Calvin are bright and special, unlike anyone else. They have a unique *essence* about them and can understand more than others. Both get feelings about things—compulsions—that guide them.

Look up *compulsion* in a dictionary. Use it in two to three sentences. Talk or write about times when you've had a compulsion that affected you.

Extension: Compare and contrast compulsions with ESP, extrasensory perception.

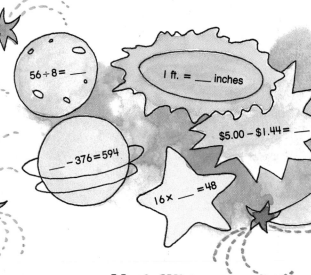

$56 \div 8 =$ ___

1 ft. = ___ inches

$5.00 - $1.44 =$ ___

___ $- 376 = 594$

$16 \times$ ___ $= 48$

Math Whiz

Meg is a whiz at math. Show your math expertise by filling in math equations on these planets.

Note to Teacher: If you laminate the planets and program them with a permanent marker, they can be wiped clean using hairspray.

Heard On The Grapevine

The Murry family lived in a small town. Anything that happened was everyone's news. The postmistress told townspeople about Mrs. Murry's unanswered letters to her missing husband. Everyone assumed that Charles Wallace was not very intelligent, because he rarely talked to them.

Discuss how and why these gossipy items got started. Then talk about how family support and understanding can overcome them. Have you ever been hurt by a rumor?

And The Greatest Of These Is LOVE

Meg learned that love was the only way to conquer IT on the planet, Camazotz. She gained strength from love thanks to all of these characters:

- her mother waiting for her father
- Charles Wallace understanding mother and her
- Calvin taking care of her
- Which, Whatsit, and Who guiding her
- Aunt Beast in its warm, caring tenderness

Think about all of the people who love you. List as many as you can, with special ways in which they show their love. Then write what you think LOVE is in a story or poem.

Fantasy Sentence Scramble

Put the words below each sentence in alphabetical order in the blanks to make complete sentences. Then read them for a summary of *A Wrinkle in Time* by Madeleine L'Engle.

1. Mrs. Whatsit is _____ _____ _____ Charles _____.
   influencing   Wallace   a   friend

2. _____, the _____ _____, measures _____ as a math _____.
   sister   Meg   up   oldest   whiz

3. Meg _____ _____ Wallace _____ Calvin _____ _____ day in the _____.
   woods   meet   and   summer   one   Charles

4. In an old _____, _____ Who _____ famous _____ and _____ _____.
   sayings   quotes   house   speedily   Mrs.   sews

5. _____ five _____ traveled by _____ _____ the _____.
   tesseract   universe   all   characters   through

6. _____ Mrs. Who _____, her tremendous _____ _____.
   twinkle   materializes   as   spectacles

7. The _____ Medium _____ as _____ _____ into her crystal ball.
   laughs   Happy   stares   she

8. On _____, Mr. Murry is being _____ _____ by IT, a _____ brain.
   wicked   prisoner   held   Camazotz

9. IT _____ and _____ _____ _____ on the _____, Camazotz.
   planet   dominates   lives   controls   everyone's

10. _____ _____ _____ _____, confused Meg.
    Beast   for   little   Aunt   her   cares

11. _____, _____, and _____ _____ _____ to escape the power of IT.
    quickly   Calvin   tesser   Meg   Father

12. _____, Meg returns to _____ to _____ _____, little Charles _____.
    rescue   alone   Wallace   Camazotz   special

Charlotte's Web

E.B. White weaves a wonderful tale about a little pig named Wilbur and his true friend, Charlotte, a spider who lives above his pigpen. With the help of Templeton, a gluttonous rat, and a brilliant plan of her own, Charlotte saves Wilbur from the fate of most barnyard pigs. Enhance the joy of reading *Charlotte's Web* with these activities.

Claudia D. Vurnakes
Summerfield, NC

Friendship Album

Wilbur and Charlotte share a deep, special friendship built on positive traits each sees in the other. They also understand each other's negative aspects. As Wilbur says in chapter 5, "But what a gamble friendship is!" Reread that passage, and discuss the pleasures and perils of finding new friends. Compile a friendship album of students' thoughts on the subject. Some starters:

Traits of the Perfect Friend
How to Wreck a Friendship
Secret Letter to an Unnamed Friend

Find That Fact!

Woven into *Charlotte's Web* are factual traits of spiders (see chapters 5, 7, 9, 13). For library detective work, have students prepare a bibliography to document each fact. First develop with the class a basic list of facts about spiders. Students write these facts on index cards, one to a card. Next they locate each fact in a reference in the library and write down the title, volume, publisher, date of publication, and page number.

Math Webs

Run off blank spiderweb sheets for quick math dri Distribute them and call out six numbers which students write in the center. Next call out a number and an operation for the spider. Students write that number and operation on the spider and use it to arrive at answers for each space on the web.

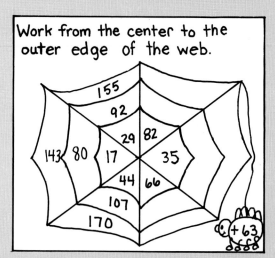

Work from the center to the outer edge of the web.

155
92
29 82
143 80 17 35
44 66
107
170

+ 63

The Joy Of Eating

In this tale, E.B. White communicates an enjoyment of food: Wilbur's list of morsels in his meals, Charlotte's love of bugs' blood, Templeton's night at the County Fair. Have students locate these passages, then think and write about food. Caution: this may be hazardous to your waistline!

Food descriptions in *Charlotte's Web* are written from the animals' points of view. We may not think Wilbur's food is delicious, but we certainly understand that Wilbur does. Write what other animals feel about their foods:

—a cat and a smelly can of cat food
—a dog and a bowl of dry dog chow
—a bird and worms

Friendship Bulletin Board

Use a bulletin board to focus on friendship. Pin or staple lengths of black yarn to the board to form a web. Students write essays on friendship to pin to the web.

Charlotte's Dictionary

From her very first greeting, Charlotte's vocabulary is impressive. Talking with her is an education for Wilbur, because she explains her words. As a fanciful vocabulary activity, challenge students to make a dictionary that Charlotte might use. Put no limits on size or materials; just require a section for each word Charlotte explains. Students must give the word, Charlotte's definition, and a sentence of their own, using the word. Be prepared for unusual-looking dictionaries!

Web Art

Combine art and geometry in a spin-off activity. Provide corrugated cardboard, string, thumbtacks, rulers, protractors, and compasses. Students choose a geometric shape and design a string web based on the shape. Encourage accuracy in drawing the designs.

Another interesting art activity involves finding an actual spiderweb. Place a sheet of dark-colored construction paper behind the web and spray gently with light-colored spray paint. The web will be preserved on paper!

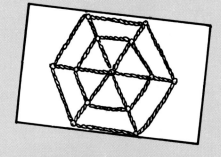

Life-giving Labels

Wilbur tried his best to live up to each label Charlotte wove into her web: SOME PIG, TERRIFIC, RADIANT, HUMBLE. Discuss with your class the good and bad ramifications of labels. For goal setting and personal growth, have each student pick a label by which he would like to be known and list ways to live up to that label.

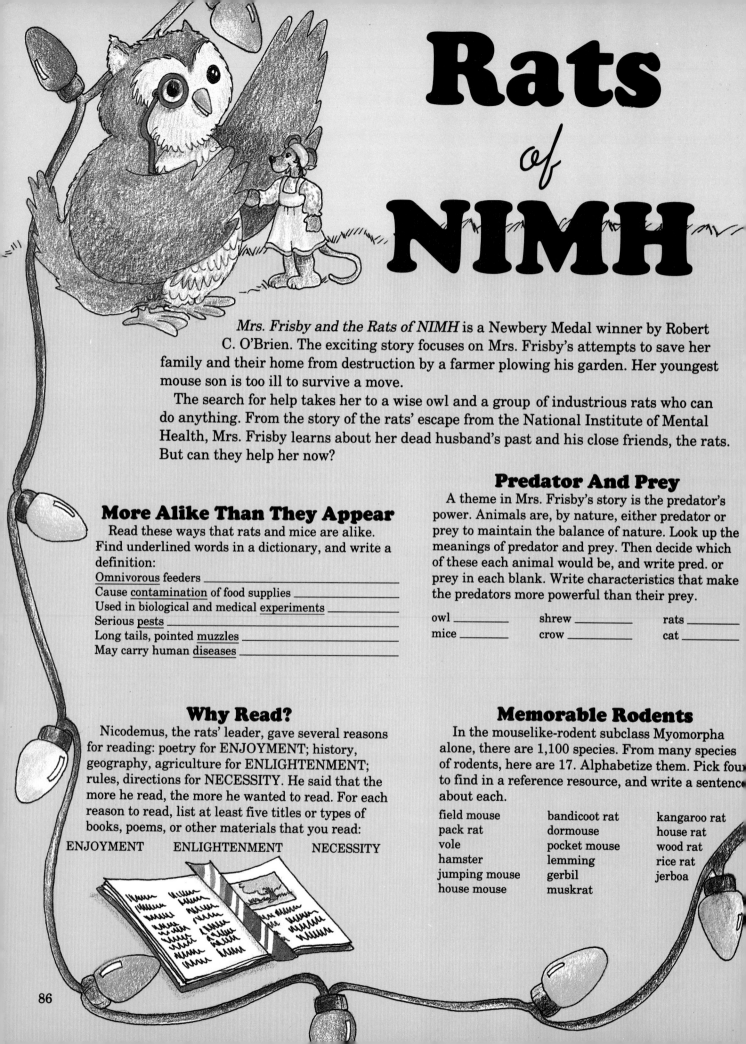

Rats of NIMH

Mrs. Frisby and the Rats of NIMH is a Newbery Medal winner by Robert C. O'Brien. The exciting story focuses on Mrs. Frisby's attempts to save her family and their home from destruction by a farmer plowing his garden. Her youngest mouse son is too ill to survive a move.

The search for help takes her to a wise owl and a group of industrious rats who can do anything. From the story of the rats' escape from the National Institute of Mental Health, Mrs. Frisby learns about her dead husband's past and his close friends, the rats. But can they help her now?

More Alike Than They Appear

Read these ways that rats and mice are alike. Find underlined words in a dictionary, and write a definition:

Omnivorous feeders _____
Cause contamination of food supplies _____
Used in biological and medical experiments _____
Serious pests _____
Long tails, pointed muzzles _____
May carry human diseases _____

Predator And Prey

A theme in Mrs. Frisby's story is the predator's power. Animals are, by nature, either predator or prey to maintain the balance of nature. Look up the meanings of predator and prey. Then decide which of these each animal would be, and write pred. or prey in each blank. Write characteristics that make the predators more powerful than their prey.

owl _____   shrew _____   rats _____
mice _____   crow _____   cat _____

Why Read?

Nicodemus, the rats' leader, gave several reasons for reading: poetry for ENJOYMENT; history, geography, agriculture for ENLIGHTENMENT; rules, directions for NECESSITY. He said that the more he read, the more he wanted to read. For each reason to read, list at least five titles or types of books, poems, or other materials that you read:

ENJOYMENT   ENLIGHTENMENT   NECESSITY

Memorable Rodents

In the mouselike-rodent subclass Myomorpha alone, there are 1,100 species. From many species of rodents, here are 17. Alphabetize them. Pick four to find in a reference resource, and write a sentence about each.

field mouse   bandicoot rat   kangaroo rat
pack rat   dormouse   house rat
vole   pocket mouse   wood rat
hamster   lemming   rice rat
jumping mouse   gerbil   jerboa
house mouse   muskrat

What Makes Someone Special?

To make a society run smoothly, each member contributes personal strengths. Characters in this story help each other by using unique abilities. After each trait and character(s) listed, write something the character(s) could perform better than the others. Be sure to use complete sentences.

TRAITS
Small size
Knowledge of local geography from the air
Leadership

Cooperation to accomplish big jobs
Medical knowledge
Engineering, construction ability
Maternal instinct for children
Advance planning

CHARACTERS
Mice (Mr. Ages, Mrs. Frisby)
The birds (The Owl and Jeremy, the Crow)
Rat (Nicodemus), Mouse (Jonathan Frisby)
Rats, rats and mice, mouse family
Mouse (Mr. Ages)
Rat (Arthur)
Mouse (Mrs. Frisby)
Rat (Nicodemus)

The Dictionary, A Fine Tool

The Toy Tinker died in the woods, so the rats used his miniature tools to make farm equipment for The Plan for their civilization. Match words below to correct guide words, and alphabetize each list—a tinker's dictionary. For extra credit, choose five words, look them up, and use them in sentences.

ables—Drills Lathes—Motors Saws—Soldering Irons Vises—Wrenches

Word List For Tinker's Dictionary:

welding tools | clamps | workbench
lubricant | wedge | lever
shears | chain | screwdrivers
lug | slide rule | sheave
winch | chisel | wire
camshaft | circular saw | machine
cog | voltmeter | servomotor
miter | differential gear | linkage
sealant | shaft | weight

Laboratory Logic

Sometimes animal lovers protest animal abuse. However, correct laboratory procedures don't allow this to happen. The rats of NIMH knew that too much time and effort had gone into experiments for their caretakers to hurt them. In each laboratory phrase, circle adjectives and underline nouns.

plastic cages
daily injections
death
clean water
teaching animals to read
painful sensations
comfortable area
plastic number-marked bands
tape recorders
progress charts

no further aging
measured food
running mazes
sickness
exercise
use of electric shocks
clipboards to take notes
faster learning ability

Those Awful Rats

Human feelings about rats come from three ideas:
1) They contaminate food supplies.
2) They may carry diseases.
3) They steal.

Take a rat's point of view, and write an essay on everything positive about rats.

Experimental Research Rats And Mice

Rats and mice are useful in research, since they get many of the same diseases as humans. Read about research involving rats to test a particular product (examples: saccharin, smoking, cancer-finding drugs, AIDS, etc.) Report to the class.

The Curse Of The Rat

Through idioms, the word "rat" has bad meanings. Translate its meaning in each phrase:

"He's a real rat fink!" _____
"I think that I smell a rat!" _____
"Ssshh! She'll rat on you to the teacher!" _____

87

Island Of The Blue Dolphins

Students are fascinated by this tale of an Indian girl, Karana, and her struggle for survival alone on a Pacific island. Weave history, science, and art into your classroom study of Scott O'Dell's award-winning book. For a related worksheet, see page 90.

Claudia D. Vurnakes
Summerfield, NC

A Look At Aloneness

Is aloneness the same as loneliness? To help students decide, have them make two lists for Karana: good and bad things about being alone on her island. Next ask the class to make similar lists for themselves. Could they manage as well as Karana did, alone for 18 years?

Rites Of Passage

When Karana and her brother were alone together on the island, Ramo decided he was the new Chief of Ghalas-at. Karana reminded him that he would have to go through the tribe's rites of manhood: a nettle-switch whipping, then being tied to a red-ant hill. Discuss modern rites of passage, like a birthday party, a bar mitzvah, and getting a driver's license. Ask small groups of students to write, then perform, passage ceremonies for major or minor milestones in kids' lives: mastering an academic or athletic skill, earning a privilege at home, getting promoted to the next grade.

The Magic Of Names

The people of Ghalas-at each had two names, a common everyday name and a secret name. Have students study first and last names of class members. As sources, use baby name books, dictionaries, encyclopedias, even oral family tradition! Students use findings to make shields or crests symbolic of their own names. Post on a bulletin board.

Pet Panorama

Karana came to feel a special friendship with the animals on her island: "Without them, the earth would be an unhappy place." Go on a library scavenger hunt for books about beloved pets. Ask students to prepare annotated bibliography cards for a Pet Panorama file. Discuss attitudes toward animals. Why do animals make good friends? Are some animals better friends than some people? Should people make friends with wild animals?

Ring Of Fire

Karana's island, San Nicolas, is located in what geologists call the Ring of Fire, the zone where three-quarters of the world's earthquakes have occurred. Assign these earthquake projects to individuals or small groups:

1. Make a map of the Ring of Fire. List what people who live in this ring should and shouldn't do before, during, and after an earthquake.
2. What do plates and faults have to do with earthquakes? What is the San Andreas Fault? How far is Karana's island from this fault?
3. Karana almost lost her life in a *tsunami,* a huge wave caused by an earthquake on the ocean floor. How is a tsunami different from effects of an earthquake on land?
4. How does a seismograph work? What is the Richter scale? A reading of 3 on the scale is how much stronger than a reading of 2?

Abstract Indian Art

Anthropologists theorized that the Indians of Karana's Pacific island migrated from the coast of Alaska since carved, painted animal figures are similar. Have students locate pictures of these abstract forms. Point out that animals were shown as if they'd been split down the middle, spread apart, and flattened. Budding artists will enjoy the challenge of applying this ancient technique to modern-day subjects: a sports car, a radio, a guitar.

Native Naturalists

Karana and her people survived on San Nicolas due to their excellent understanding of nature. Collect a set of field guides, and let students get acquainted with flora and fauna of the island. Have students fill out fact sheets for any ten of the species listed, using field guidebooks as their sources.

Fish/Shellfish	Birds	Animals
Tuna	Olivaceous Cormorant	Sea Otter
Abalone	(Karana used feathers from this	(Won-a-nee and her two babies)
Scallop	bird for her skirt.)	Red Fox
Starfish	Pelican	Blue Dolphin
Sea Urchin	Blue Jay	Whale
White Bass	Western Tanager	Seal
Devilfish	(the tame birds, Tainor and Lurai)	Sea Elephant
	Red-winged Blackbird	

Karana's Diary

What did Karana think of her new life when white men took her to live at the Mission Santa Barbara? Have students write Karana's diary. Ask them to include her reactions to inventions with which she was unfamiliar and to historical events taking place near her new home.

Island Of The Blue Dolphins

How well do you remember this terrific tale?
Finish each sentence by writing the correct number on the dolphin.

Karana lived alone on the island . . .

Karana's father was . . .

Karana's best friend on the island was . . .

Karana was left behind because . . .

A girl who came with the Aleut hunters . . .

Tainor and Lurai were . . .

Karana's fence around her house was . . .

Karana's brother, Ramo, was . . .

Karana tried to leave the island by . . .

When Karana finally left on the white men's ship, she . . .

Ulape was . . .

Karana liked her cormorant skirt better than . . .

1. . . . she jumped out of the white men's ship to be with Ramo.

2. . . . two tame otters.

3. . . . the chief of Ghalas-at.

4. . . . an Aleut hunter.

5. . . . Rontu, a wild dog she tamed.

6. . . . took Rontu-Aru and her tame birds.

7. . . . killed by a pack of wild dogs.

8. . . . Karana's older sister.

9. . . . for 18 years.

10. . . . the blue dress the white man made.

11. . . . a pair of beautiful birds Karana tamed.

12. . . . Karana's mother.

13. . . . paddling to another island in a large canoe.

14. . . . made from whale ribs and bull kelp.

15. . . . gave Karana a necklace of black stones.

TRACKING DOWN RESEARCH SKILLS

"The teacher says everyone has to write a report," moaned Randy. "I don't know where to start!" wailed Jill.

Sound familiar? If you've been searching for an easier way to teach your students how to write good reports, look no further than these activities and the reproducibles on pages 94 to 96.

Ideas by Melissa Matusevich

HOW DO I START?

Understanding how to limit the topic of a research report is sometimes difficult for students. Point out to your class that the choice of a topic often depends upon the amount of time given to prepare the report or the length of the paper. Then have students decide which topics below are suitable for a one- to two-page report.

Snakes (too broad)   Boa Constrictors (suitable)
Reptiles (too broad)   Superstitions About Snakes (too narrow)
Bodies of Snakes (suitable)   First Aid for Snake Bites (too narrow)

Limit your students' choices by having the entire class do reports on animals. (Other good categories include presidents, countries, inventors, or states.)

WHERE DO I FIND INFORMATION?

Before heading to the library, take time to review the card catalog. Explain to students that nonfiction books have three catalog cards: subject, title, and author. Using three different colors of chalk, draw an example of each type of card on the board. (See your librarian for examples). Discuss their formats; then call out each title or topic below. Have students identify the kind of card on which they would find the information. For extra practice, write this list on the board for students to alphabetize according to the order in which they would be found in the card catalog.

1. A book about beavers (subject)
2. Books by Merlin Carlson (author)
3. A book called <u>Dolphins and Porpoises</u> (title)
4. A book of pictures of snakes (subject)
5. A book called <u>Wild Birds of South America</u> (title)
6. A book of animal folktales by Miriam Wise (author)

HOW DO I TAKE NOTES?

Use your overhead projector to help students develop notetaking skills. After going over the tips shown, give each student a 3" × 5" index card. Have students take notes on a short paragraph displayed on the overhead. The next day, instruct students to write a paragraph using their notes. For additional practice, see the reproducible on page 94.

Notetaking Tips
1. Write the name of the book and the author at the beginning or on the back of your note card.
2. Read for facts. Look for the main idea of each paragraph. Write it down.
3. Add the details you want to remember. Don't copy sentences word for word.
4. Be sure your notes are accurate.
5. If you must copy a sentence directly from a book, put quotation marks around it. Note the page number.

Sample paragraph
A gorilla looks mean. It has a shiny, black face. There is a thick ridge of bone over the gorilla's eyes. Gorillas have large, pointed teeth. There is no hair on a gorilla's face. Black or dark brown hair covers all of its body except for the palms of its hands and the soles of its feet. The adult male gorilla has grayish hair on his back. This powerful ape has large shoulders, a broad chest, long arms, and short legs.

WHAT DO I DO WITH MY NOTES?

Students need to know how to organize their notes into an outline. To familiarize your class with outlining, give each child a duplicated copy of a short article (three to four paragraphs) from an encyclopedia. As a class, determine the main topics (Roman numerals) of the article. Write these on the overhead. Add the sub-topics and any details. Have students copy the finished outline to use as a guide when they get ready to organize their notes. Follow up this activity with the worksheet on page 95.

I'M READY TO WRITE!

Explain to students that they will probably make mistakes on their rough drafts. Post the Proofreading Guidelines shown. Discuss each type of error and how to mark it when editing. Then write the following paragraph on the board. Have students copy the paragraph exactly as is shown, then mark whatever corrections have to be made with red pencils or marking pens.

Proofreading Guidelines
1. Cross out each misspelled word or any word you want to replace. Write the correct word above it.
2. Add missing punctuation marks.
3. Use periods to break up run-on sentences. Remove periods after groups of words that are not sentences.
4. Put a slash (/) through a small letter that should be capitalized and through a capital letter that should be a smaller letter. Write the correct form above it.
5. Use a caret (∧) to show where a word has been left out. Write the word above it.
6. Mark out any word, sentence, or phrase that isn't needed.
7. Use ¶ to show that a new paragraph should be started.

Australa has many unusual birds The emu is Australias largest bird it is Fast runner. The emu can't fly. another flightless bird is the Australian penguin. it is only ten inches high. Kangaroos are found in Australia. The kookaburra Can fly, but it cant sing Insteed, it makes a. laughing sounnd

FIVE DAYS TO A
FIRST-RATE REPORT

Organize yourself and your students with the help of this practical five-day plan.

PREPARATION

1. Post a list of animal topics. Have each student sign up for an animal.
2. Gather reference books, filmstrips and viewers, and other resources.
3. Have each child make a folder from construction paper to use as storage for note cards, outlines, and other materials. Allow students time to decorate their folders with pictures of their animals.
4. Give each student ten to 15 index cards for notetaking.
5. Duplicate "My Report Checklist" on page 96 for each child. Have students staple the checklists inside their folders.

DAY 1

Combine notetaking and outlining in one step. Post the sample outline. Have students label one index card for each subtopic, then write their notes on the appropriate cards. (Students can put bibliographic information on the backs of the cards.)

Sample Outline

Animal _____

I. Physical Description
   A. Size, shape, and color
   B. Surface covering
   C. Other unusual characteristics

II. Habitat And Lifestyle
   A. Shelter and environment
   B. Food
   C. Family life

III. Adaptations
   A. Tools for defense
   B. Uses by man
   C. Other unusual characteristics

I. A. Size, shape, and color

I. B. Surface covering

Sample note cards

DAY 2

Use the sample outline to help children organize their note cards in the proper order. Tell them to use the information from each card to write a paragraph of their report. Have students copy their bibliographic information on a separate sheet of paper.

DAY 3

Edit rough drafts in class. For an extra check, allow each student to swap his report with an "editing partner."

DAY 4

Let students recopy their reports in their best handwriting. Provide art paper and supplies. Have each student design and make a cover for his report.

End the week with a "Sharing Day." Have students place their reports on their desks. Allow each child to change desks with a friend to read his report. Have students change desks again after two to three minutes. Continue until each child has read at least five different reports. Then place the reports in a laundry basket or box for lots of free-time reading!

All You Need Are Notes!

When you prepare a report, your notes should be a brief summary of important information, <u>not</u> sentences copied word for word. After you choose a topic, make an outline. Then, fill in the outline with information from books, encyclopedias, or other reference sources.

Directions: Read the paragraph; then fill in the outline.

The beaver is known for its wide, flat tail. This tail is used to steer when the beaver swims. Beavers have strong front teeth for cutting trees. They use tree branches to build dams and *lodges* (homes) in the rivers and streams where they live. Beavers live in groups called *colonies*. A beaver's diet consists of bark, twigs, leaves, and roots of trees and shrubs. The young beavers are called *kits* or *pups*. After birth, kits stay with the adults for two years. Then, they are sent away from the family.

I.   Body of a beaver

    A. <u>Known for wide, flat tail</u>

    B. _____

    C. _____

II. Where beavers live

    A. _____

    B. _____

III. Diet of beavers

    A. _____

    B. _____

    C. _____

    D. _____

IV. Young beavers

    A. _____

    B. _____

    C. _____

Now fold this sheet so that the paragraph is hidden. Use your notes to write your own paragraph about beavers on another sheet of paper.

Ready To Write

The example below shows how to use an outline to write a report.
Study the sample outline and report; then follow these steps.

1. Pick a topic from an encyclopedia.
2. Write an outline for the topic on the blanks below.
3. Use your outline to write a report about your topic on another sheet of paper.

The California Condor

I. Appearance
   A. Wingspan of 8 to 10 feet
   B. Black feathers
   C. White area under wings
   D. Red-orange neck and head
   E. No feathers on head and neck

II. Habits
   A. Eats remains of dead animals
   B. Does not build nests
   C. Powerful, graceful flier

III. Habitat
   A. Found in southern California
   B. Has nearly died out
   C. Lives in protected areas

The California Condor

California condors have a wingspan of eight to ten feet. Their bodies are mostly covered with black feathers except for a white area on the underside of the wings. Their necks and heads are red-orange. Condors have no feathers on their heads and necks.

Condors eat the remains of dead animals. Condors are unusual because they do not build nests. Soaring and gliding for long distances, condors are known as powerful and graceful fliers.

Did you know that the California condor is found mostly in southern California? Since they have nearly died out, most surviving condors live in protected areas.

Topic: _____

I. _____

   A. _____

   B. _____

   C. _____

II. _____

   A. _____

   B. _____

   C. _____

III. _____

   A. _____

   B. _____

   C. _____

Bonus Box: Draw a picture to go with your report.

My Report Checklist

Topic of report: _____ Due date: _____

Directions: Check off each step as you complete it.

Day I

_____ 1. Label your index cards using the sample outline given to you by your teacher.

_____ 2. Choose resource books or encyclopedias from which to take notes. (Ask your teacher or librarian if you need help.)

_____ 3. Write notes from your reading on the index cards. Don't forget to write bibliographic information on the back of each card.

Day 2

_____ 1. Use the sample outline to put your index cards in the right order.

_____ 2. Write a title for your report at the top of a sheet of paper.

_____ 3. Use the information from each card to write one paragraph for your report.

_____ 4. List the bibliographic information from the backs of the cards on a separate sheet of paper. Don't forget that a bibliography is organized in alphabetical order. Title this page "Bibliography."

Day 3

_____ 1. Edit your rough draft.

_____ 2. Have a friend or family member read your rough draft. Make any necessary changes.

Day 4

_____ 1. Recopy your report in your best handwriting.

_____ 2. Make a cover for your report.

_____ 3. Cut out or draw a picture to illustrate your topic. Place the picture after the last page of your report (before the bibliography).

Day 5

_____ 1. Share your report with your classmates.

_____ 2. Write a paragraph telling how you feel about your report. What do you like about it? What would you change? What was the most difficult step in writing your report? The easiest? Give your paragraph to your teacher.

Best of *THE MAILBOX* • *INTERMEDIATE* • ©The Education Center, Inc. • Melissa Matusevich, Blacksburg, VA

Note to teacher: Use this sheet with "Five Days To A First-Rate Report" on **page 93.**

Back-To-School Bonuses
What To Do With Your Kids On The First Days Of School

Ideas by Melissa Matusevich

WANTED: New Students

Welcome your new crew with fact-filled "WANTED" posters. Write important information about each student (gathered from school records or last year's teachers) on a duplicated "WANTED" poster. Place the posters on a large bulletin board. Students will enjoy reading about each other on the first day back at school. Have students add photos from home and other pertinent information about themselves as the week progresses.

Back-To-School Raps

Older students enjoy listening to Top 40 tunes on the radio. Many of these include rhythmic conversations called rapping. Introduce your students to the year ahead with a toe-tapping, back-to-school rap. Begin by duplicating the following rap. Have several students recite the rap in unison, teaching it to the rest of the class.

Divide your class into groups. Give each group a textbook you will use during the year. Have each group review their book and write a rap describing its topics. Hold a "Rap Session" for groups to perform their raps for their classmates.

Back To School

Well, it's really cool
'Cause we're back in school.
We're going to study hard
So we won't be fools.
The subjects we'll learn just can't be beat,
and we'll always be sure our work is neat.
There'll be math, social studies,
Science and art,
Writing, spelling, and health
Will play a big part.
Music, reading, and English will be part of our day,
And when we're finished, we'll go out to play!
So we'd better get busy 'cause it's time to begin,
So we can be smarter when this year ends!

Me Books

Getting to know your students is easy with "Me Books." Give each student 13 blank pages for his book. Post titles for the pages on the board. Have children copy a title at the top of each page. Students write several sentences and add illustrations on each page. Let students bind their books in bright, construction paper covers. Put the books in a large basket at your reading center for everyone to enjoy — including you!

Titles

I Was Born!
My Family
My Favorites (color, food, animal, etc.)
My Favorite Outdoor Activity
My Favorite Indoor Activity
My Favorite Clothes and Foods
What I Like To Do With My Friends

What I Like To Do Alone
What Makes Me Feel Important
What Makes Me Happy
What Makes Me Sad
Three People I Admire And Why
My Most Embarrassing Moment

Getting-Acquainted Cards

Help new students get over the "first-day jitters" with this activity. Label a set of cards with statements such as "I was born in a foreign country" or "I have an unusual pet." In turn, read each card orally. Any student to which the card applies stands up and gives the class more information.

Sample cards
I am an only child.
I play on a Little League sports team.
My mother has an unusual job.
My father has an unusual job.
I have traveled outside of this state.
I have met a famous person.
I read an interesting book this summer.

I have earned my own money.

It's In The Bag!

Help your students get to know one another with an interviewing activity. Write each child's name on a small paper bag. Staple the bags to a bulletin board with the title, "_____ Grade — It's In The Bag!" Place the name of a classmate inside each bag. Have a few students at a time remove their bags from the board. Each child pulls the name from his bag and spends a few minutes interviewing that classmate. On the board, write a list of good questions to ask:

Where were you born?
Who are the other members of your family?
What are your hobbies?
What is the most interesting place you've ever visited?
What is your favorite movie?
How do you like to spend a Saturday afternoon?

Set aside time for each student to "introduce" the interviewee to the rest of the class.

Hangman Math Game

Play "Stop The Hangman" to assess math skills. Divide the class into four teams. Draw a "hangman" on the chalkboard for each team. Call out a math problem for the teams to solve. The first team to answer correctly erases part of their hangman. (Be sure all the students on the team have worked the problem.) The first team to completely erase their "hangman" wins. Use a math book from the students' previous grade as a source for problems.

Classroom Bingo

Duplicate two copies of the sheet on page 99 for each student. Have children completely fill in both of their copies. (Be sure the copies are filled in identically.) Cut one copy apart, and place the pieces in a box. Mount the other copy on a piece of construction paper, and laminate. Use popcorn kernels as markers. To play, draw a piece from the box and call it out. Anyone with a match covers it on his card. The first person with bingo wins. To vary, have students trade cards with a friend — a great way to get to know someone else! Save this game for the rainy or snowy days ahead.

Wall Of Fame

Induct your new students into a "Wall of Fame." Divide a large bulletin board into sections, one for each student. During the first week of school, let each child decorate his section with personal items — baby pictures, hobby items, family snapshots, original drawings. Classmates will be amazed at how much they can learn about their old and new friends from this attractive display.

Back-To-School Reproducibles

Duplicate the reproducible sheets on pages 99-101 before students arrive so they'll be ready to use at a moment's notice. Have each student staple his copy of the contract on page 181 to a file folder. Students can store finished contract work inside their folders. Send the parent notices on page 101 home with students during the first week.

CLASSROOM BINGO

Month of my birthday	My favorite color	My favorite animal	Color of my house	Color of my parents' car
My favorite toy	My favorite food	Number of sisters	Color of my room	My favorite school subject
My teacher last year	My favorite book	My favorite song	My favorite TV show	My favorite sport
My favorite board game	My phone number	My favorite movie	My favorite rock group/star	Any number from 1 to 100
My best friend	My favorite flower	Number of brothers	What I want to be when I grow up	My favorite hobby

Fill in each square on your card. Color the card.

Note to teacher: Duplicate two copies per student. See the game instructions on page 98.

Getting To Know You

Fill in the blanks. If you need more space, use the back of this sheet.

1. Number of people in your family: _____

2. Number of brothers: _____ Number of sisters: _____

3. Do you have any pets? _____ Describe them: _____
   _____

4. List any jobs you do at home each week:
   _____, _____, _____

5. If you had an entire day to do anything you'd like, how would you spend
   that day? _____
   _____

6. Pretend you can invite <u>any</u> person in the world to be your teacher for one
   week. Who would you invite? List three people: _____
   _____, _____, _____

7. What do you consider your best school subject? _____

8. List your "favorites":

   food: _____   sport to play: _____

   color: _____   sport to watch: _____

   TV show: _____   hobby: _____

   book (title): _____ school subject: _____

9. Pretend you have written a book. What kind of book is it? (history, fiction,
   biography, etc.) _____
   On the back of this sheet, tell what the book is about.

10. On the back of this sheet, write anything else you would like to tell about
    yourself.

Best of THE MAILBOX ● INTERMEDIATE ● ©The Education Center, Inc.

Dear Parents,

Our class needs the circled art materials. Can you help us?

egg cartons
spools
newspapers
sponges
baby food jars
Popsicle sticks

Styrofoam trays
pipe cleaners
yarn
wallpaper samples
paper plates
gift wrap

cotton balls
fabric scraps
ribbon
glitter
greeting cards
paper or plastic bags

S.O.S.

Thank you! _____

(teacher)

Note to teacher: Circle the items you need on the memo. Duplicate it and send it home with students.

A WEEK'S WORTH OF WORK!

Student: _____

Date: _____

Dear Parents,
   Please look over your child's weekly papers. Sign this note and have your child return it to school. Please keep the papers. Thank you.
                    Sincerely,
                    Teacher: _____

Parent signature: _____

Comments:

_____

_____

Note to teacher: Have each student store his graded papers in a folder. Duplicate this memo. At the end of the week, staple the memo to each child's papers. Students return the signed memo for you to check.

Paula Holdren, Prospect, KY

OPENING NIGHT

It's that time of the year again—Open House Night at your school! New students, new teachers, new parents!

What's in store when school doors open to the inquisitive crowds? Be prepared for rave reviews when you use these Open House ideas!

Me Mobiles

Decorate the room with "Me Mobiles" hanging from the ceiling. Each student writes his name on a piece of colored construction paper. Children slip the colored papers over their hangers and attach items that describe themselves or things that they enjoy.

Paula K. Holdren
Prospect, KY

Award-Winning Badges

Have a school-wide contest for students to design badges for visitors. Students or teachers can vote for the winning design. Duplicate the "official" badges, and let children color them. This whole-school effort will be very satisfying.

Sr. Ann Claire Rhoads
Emmitsburg, MD

Sign Up, Please!

Looking for parent volunteers for field trips, class parties, and clerical tasks? Design a display that they can't miss at Open House! Place an attractive booklet and several pens in an area of the classroom. Invite parents to sign up for the jobs they would like. It will save you countless hours on the telephone searching for last-minute help.

Paula K. Holdren

Parents and Students Are Winners!

As the parents enter the classroom, have them sign up for a door prize to be given the next day in class. The prize can be a flower, a book, a plaque, or another inexpensive item. The parents enjoy it, and the children are excited to see who wins.

Sr. Margaret Ann Wooden
Martinsburg, WV

Student Dummies?

Welcome parents with a classroom full of student dummies! Have each child lie down on a piece of butcher paper. Trace around him, and let him color and cut out his outline. Put each outlined form in the child's desk. Will parents be able to find their child's place?

Kathy Beard
Keystone Heights, FL

Valentine's Day Party
Date: February 14
Time: 1:00
Cupcakes/cookies _____
Drinks _____
Cups and napkins _____

Classroom Newspaper
Date: October 15
Typing _____

Open House Mobiles

The key to a successful Open House is to provide as many displays of children's work as possible. Parents want to see their child's work, not just the best papers in the class. Over each child's desk, hang a low mobile to display work in different subject areas. Have each student mount samples of his schoolwork on both sides of pieces of construction paper. Be sure each mobile is balanced before hanging.

Katie Baily
Avon, CT

Open House Posters

To make an Open House display that's a knockout, give each student a piece of brightly colored poster board to make a personal poster of his interests and achievements. Choose an appropriate title for each child's poster such as Abby's Attic, Brian's Box, and Jimmy's Jeans. Children fill their posters with photos of themselves and their families, autobiographies, worksheets from every school subject, awards, artwork, and momentos. Display these in the hall for all to see.

Gerry Scobel
Zelienople, PA

Open House Invitation

Write an invitation to Open House on the board. Use it as a handwriting assignment. Children will do their best when they know it's going home to Mom and Dad!

Kathy Beard
Keystone Heights, FL

Class Video Stars

Videotape a class play or lesson to play back on Open House Night. The kids will love the experience of being on TV and will beg their parents to come see the video show. Each child is involved, and parents will leave smiling after seeing their "little ones" on TV!

Francine Reinel
Sarasota, FL

All About Me

As they present these books to parents at Open House, children can proudly say, "Here's a book all about me!" Watch as children and parents sit down to turn the pages together. Have students begin work on their books on the first day of school. Each day, hand out pages for children to fill in with information about themselves. Topics may include: Interests, Favorites, Special Feelings, Dreams, Things That Bug Me, My Autobiography, Family Tree, Places I Have Lived, Places I Have Visited, Family, School, and Weekends. Bind each student's pages together to make a unique book and a special gift that is sure to impress parents.

Julia K. Mozingo
Altus, OK

A Welcoming Committee of One

If your Open House comes in the fall, a scarecrow may be just the thing to welcome family and friends to your classroom. Students will have fun building a scarecrow from an old lamp stand and adding clothes stuffed with straw or newspaper. Let classmates name their class mascot. Give him a sign, place him by the door to welcome guests, and add a few pumpkins at his feet. Visitors can't miss your classroom with this charming fellow to meet and greet them!

Lynda Holding
Blanchard, OK

Create Classroom Atmosphere

During Open House, set a calm, pleasant atmosphere by playing soft, recorded music at a low volume. Flowers and plants add a touch of "class" to the classroom, too.

Kelley Dean
Parkin, AR

Welcome to Mrs. Meyer's Class

Catch That Football Fever!

Kick off football season with these activities and the reproducibles on pages 106 and 107. You'll score points with your students as they tackle basic skills.

Cheers For The Home Team

Football fans in 28 cities in the United States can cheer for a home team. Have students locate these teams on a U.S. map. Look at a fall game schedule (check your local newspaper's sports page), and use yarn to connect cities to show the week's opposing teams.

National Conference
Atlanta Falcons
Chicago Bears
Dallas Cowboys
Detroit Lions
Green Bay Packers
Los Angeles Rams
Minnesota Vikings
New Orleans Saints
New York Giants
Philadelphia Eagles
San Francisco 49ers
St. Louis Cardinals
Tampa Bay Buccaneers
Washington Redskins

American Conference
Buffalo Bills
Cincinnati Bengals
Cleveland Browns
Denver Broncos
Houston Oilers
Indianapolis Colts
Kansas City Chiefs
Los Angeles Raiders
Miami Dolphins
New England Patriots
New York Jets
Pittsburgh Steelers
San Diego Chargers
Seattle Seahawks

SPORTS◆NEWS

The Sports Page

Want kids to cheer for capitalization and punctuation practice? With the help of your local newspaper's sports page, they will! Cut out headlines and sentences from articles reporting national and local team news. Rewrite on poster board strips, leaving out all capital letters and punctuation marks. Place strips in a football helmet at your language arts center. Students take a strip and rewrite the sentence correctly on their paper.

the dallas
cowboys will
play glenn high
lost the game
at fairview

MEMBER OF THE CHAMPIONSHIP

READING TEAM!

Training Camp For Readers

This training camp encourages varied preseason reading. Children earn a place on the class reading team by completing the book contract on page 106. Each child reads and records titles of books. Award students who complete their contract with season passes, good for ten visits to the library.

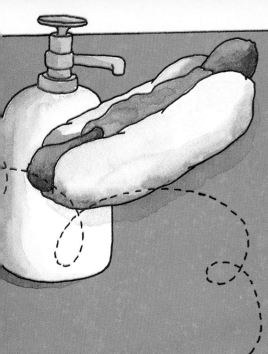

Hot Dogs, All The Way!

Bite into some economics to discover what's behind a hot dog stand at a football game. Have student groups research wholesale prices for hot dogs, rolls, mustard, and ketchup. (Check with a local grocer.) Groups then calculate costs and profits based on average attendance figures from last year's season. Contact the principal of a local high school for this information. Next have students determine a price per hot dog and submit a bid to you. After naming each "Hot Dog Enterprise," compare group costs on a chart to see who can produce the cheapest, yummiest hot dogs.

Most Valuable Players

Watch these most valuable players! Use this bulletin board to express pride in your winning team! Use the pattern on page 108 to make construction paper helmets. Each week award helmets to students who have earned them with good work or behavior. Students decorate their helmets and mount them on the board.

Spelling Coaches

Make spelling drills more fun by assigning spelling coaches each week. The coach's job is to get his team (three to four other students) in shape for the weekly spelling "play-off." Coaches may call out the words for the week to their teams or have students practice with these categories:

Spell a word with a silent letter.   Spell a word that rhymes with . . .   Spell a word that means . . .

Look Into The Football Future

For a fun end-of-the-unit activity, have students predict the winner of this year's Super Bowl. Give each student a copy of the football pattern on page 108. Students write their predictions on their footballs, naming the National Football Conference team and the American Conference team they believe will meet in the 1989 Super Bowl, and who will win. Collect helmets and store in a safe place until the day after Super Bowl Sunday. Even your less-than-enthusiastic football fans will enjoy the anticipation of discovering whose "crystal ball" was correct.

Be A 100-Yard Reader!

Each book is worth ten yards. When you finish a book, check the correct box below and write the title on a ten-yard line. Fill in the entire field and you'll score a reading touchdown!

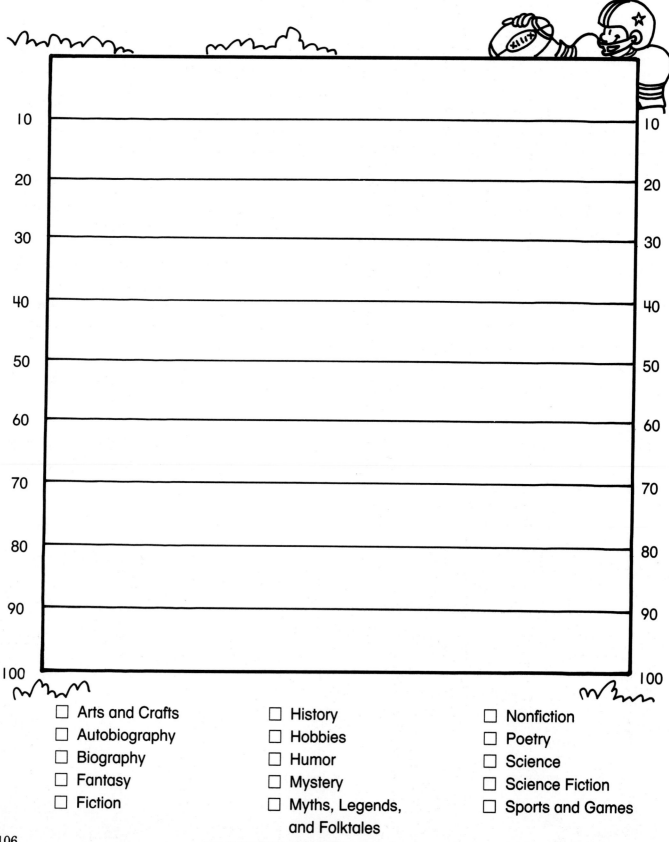

☐ Arts and Crafts   ☐ History   ☐ Nonfiction
☐ Autobiography   ☐ Hobbies   ☐ Poetry
☐ Biography   ☐ Humor   ☐ Science
☐ Fantasy   ☐ Mystery   ☐ Science Fiction
☐ Fiction   ☐ Myths, Legends,   ☐ Sports and Games
                        and Folktales

Name _____

Football Gear

Work the problems on the back of this sheet.
Write your answers in the numbered footballs below.

1. The equipment manager bought 22 pairs of socks at $2.00 per pair. How much did he spend on socks?

2. The first aid kit had 40 bandages. The team doctor used 10 at one game, 14 at another, and then 4 more. How many bandages are left?

3. The locker room manager collected 7 bags of dirty laundry. Each one weighed about 25 pounds. About how many pounds of laundry were collected?

4. The team used 308 towels last week. This week they used 267 towels. How many more towels were used last week?

5. A team carries 2,500 pounds of equipment along to a road game. How many trunks are needed if each trunk holds 100 pounds?

6. It takes 3 feet of adhesive tape for the trainer to wrap one ankle. How much tape is used to wrap 9 ankles?

7. Knee pads cost $8.65 per pair. Shoulder pads cost $60.98 each. How much more do shoulder pads cost?

8. A team spends over $600.00 to equip each player. How much does it spend for 5 players?

9. Each player has a duffel bag weighing about 56 pounds. How many pounds of equipment are there in 4 bags?

10. Each player needs a pair of mud cleats and a pair of rubber-soled shoes for icy fields. Mud cleats cost $35.95. Rubber-soled shoes cost $42.75. How much for both pairs?

11. A football helmet costs $78.50. How much do 9 helmets cost?

12. Football jerseys cost $15.00 each. How much will it cost to buy enough for 9 players?

Patterns

See the activities for using these patterns on pages 104 and 105.

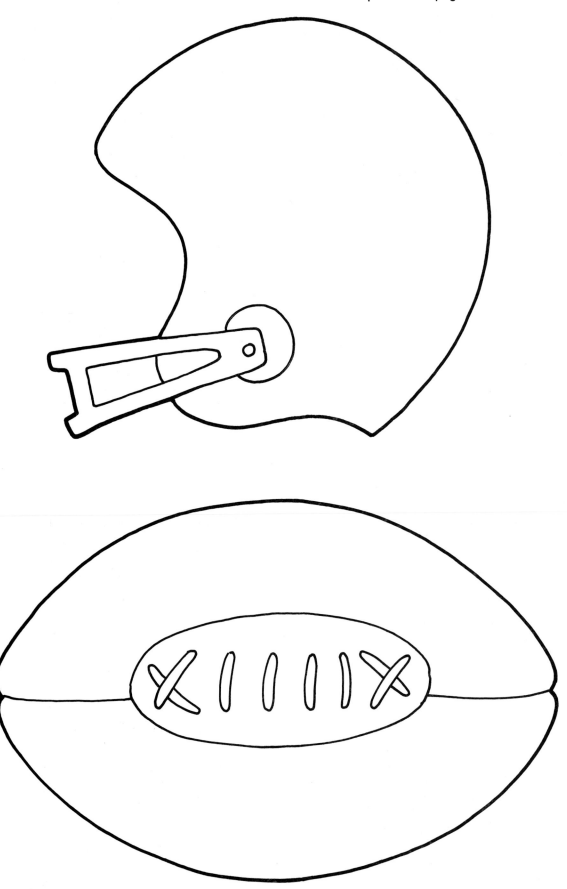

Our Daily Bread

The Food and Agriculture Organization of the United Nations estimates that up to 450 million people suffer from hunger and undernutrition. Due to poverty, changes in crop yield, population, and/or cultural habits, 12 countries see hunger on a vast scale. With estimates of their undernourished rounded in millions, they are: India (201); Indonesia (33); Bangladesh (27); Nigeria (14); Brazil, Ethiopia, and Pakistan (12 each); Philippines (10); Afghanistan (6); Burma, Colombia, and Thailand (5 each). **Alert children to the true value of their daily bread with these activities on World Food Day in October.**

Some impoverished children survive by eating what they find in garbage cans. After students list what would be in a day's worth of trash at home, have them describe the meal they could have from it.

Susan Layne
Bedford, VA

Have each student record the food his family wastes in one week. Then estimate the cost of the food, and multiply the amount by 52. What is the yearly total?

Susan Layne

Treat your class to a symbol and food company match-up! Paste logos from well-known food products on a sturdy shopping bag and number. Students number their papers and write company names before checking with a key.

The average person in India lives on $150 per year. That means a family of eight would live on $1,200 a year or $100 per month. Divide students into small groups to pretend they are families in India. Have them plan a monthly budget, allowing for food, clothing, shelter, transportation, and medical bills.

Susan Layne

Another listing activity will give children an idea of how much money is spent on junk food. Instruct students to make a daily list of soft drinks, chips, and candy bars that they eat. At the end of one week, total the amounts. Then multiply by 52 to find the approximate yearly cost. How many people could that amount feed for a period of time?

Susan Layne

Some people live on one cup of rice per day. Let students try this experiment for a day to find out what that's like. Eat only ⅓ cup of cooked rice and water for each meal. (No snacks between meals!) Have them write a paragraph describing their feelings throughout the day.

Susan Layne

Students will have to put their thinking caps on to become "The Wizards of Eetz"! These wizards have the power to erase world hunger. Have children list and explain causes of hunger, then tell what they would have to do to eliminate each.

R_x FOR PERKY PUNCTUATION

What do you do when your students' punctuation skills begin to lag? Perk them up, of course! Shape up important punctuation basics with these activities and the reproducibles on pages 112 and 113.

Ideas by Sue Nations

EYE CHART

. , ! ? ; : - " "

. , ! ? ; : - " "

. ! ? ; : - " "

. ! ? ; : - " "

. , ! ? ; : - " "

. , ! ? ; : - " "

The Difference Commas Make

Commas <u>do</u> make a difference—sometimes the difference between life and death, as this incident shows:

> By moving a single comma in a warrant which had been signed by her husband, the wife of a czar saved the life of an accused man. The man was to be sent to Siberia to be executed. The warrant read, "Pardon impossible, to be sent to Siberia." The czar's wife, wishing to save the man, changed the punctuation so that the warrant read, "Pardon, impossible to be sent to Siberia." The man was set free.

After sharing this account with your students, have them write original sentences and change their meanings by altering the placement of commas. Or challenge students to search in books, magazines, and newspapers to find sentences with meanings which are dependent upon the placement of commas. Have students share their sentences by copying them on a large class chart.

Book Reports That Hit The Mark!

Get twice the mileage out of punctuation practice with this book report project. Give each student a large index card. On the card, the student writes the title, author, and ten sentences from the book, omitting all punctuation. Challenge students to search for sentences which will entice someone to read the book. The student also writes an answer key on the back of the card.

Collect the cards and use them for class practice sessions or at a center for free-time use. Students will receive punctuation practice and reading recommendations all at the same time!

You Don't Say

Students have opinions about lots of things, so why not put them to good punctuation use? Post student photos or self-portraits on a bulletin board entitled "You Don't Say!" Have each student cut out a speech bubble and label it with his opinion about a current topic. Mount the bubbles above the appropriate pictures. Use the display to provide lots of personalized practice with quotation marks. Have students rewrite each opinion as a direct quotation (see example). Change the board by having students write new speech bubbles about a different topic.

Christmas vacation should last for one whole month!

Jackson

Example:
Jackson declared, "Christmas vacation should last for one whole month!"

PRESCRIPTION FOR PERKY PUNCTUATION

Use a comma:
1. to separate items in a series: I like apples, oranges, and limes.
2. to separate the names of cities, states, and countries.
3. to separate the day of the month and the year.
4. after the greeting of a friendly letter and the closing of any letter.
5. to set off the name of a person who is addressed in a sentence:
    Cindy, will you close the door?
6. to set off introductory words like *yes* and *no*.
7. to separate an appositive from the rest of the sentence:
    Marian, a soccer player, spoke to our class.
8. before the conjunction in a compound sentence:
    Joe ran in the race, but Harvey kept the time clock.
9. to set off an introductory clause from the rest of the sentence:
    After we had packed the car, we went inside for supper.
10. to set off an interrupting phrase: Skiing, I believe, is an exciting sport.
11. to separate adjectives that are not joined by a conjunction:
    That laughing, jolly clown makes me giggle.
12. to separate a direct quotation from the rest of the sentence:
    "Pass me the book," Harvey asked.
    "That story," Jean said, "is funny!"

Use quotation marks:
1. to enclose the exact words of a speaker.
2. around the titles of poems, plays, stories, and songs.

Use a colon:
1. in writing times: It is now 6:45.
2. before a list or series:
    There were three winners: Sara, Britt, Mark.
3. after the greeting in a business letter.
4. to separate the chapter and verse in a biblical reference:
    Proverbs 3:5.
5. to show the speaker in a play or dialogue:
    Greg: What time did he leave?

Use a semicolon:
1. between the independent clauses of a compound sentence when a conjunction is not used:
    Elaine washed the dog; Allen dried him off.

Use a hyphen:
1. to divide a word between syllables at the end of a line.
2. to join parts of some compound words: drive-in, mother-in-law.
3. to write number words from 21 through 99: twenty-one.

Note To Teacher: Post this sheet on a punctuation bulletin board or duplicate a copy for each of your students.

Just What The Doctor Ordered

R **Use a comma:**
1. to separate items in a series: He plays tennis, soccer, and golf.
2. to separate the names of cities, states, and countries.
3. to separate the day of the month and the year.
4. after the greeting of a friendly letter and the closing of any letter.
5. to set off the name of a person who is addressed in a sentence: Howie, will you open the present?
6. to set off introductory words like *yes* and *no*.
7. to separate an appositive from the rest of the sentence: Jillian, my best friend, has the flu.

Directions:
You'll find ten animal names hidden in these sentences and the letter!
Add commas where needed; then circle the names of the hidden animals.
The first one has been done for you.

1. Ann, did you help plan the annual picnic?

2. Tom Sales our fire chief said that the cause of the fire might be arson.

3. Yes I saw a famous entertainer when I visited Hollywood California.

4. How long does it take to drive from Mobile Alabama to St. Louis Missouri?

5. The sound of the echo goes bouncing from the hillside to the canyon and to the valley below.

6. The students wanted to go to Del Rio Texas or Acapulco Mexico.

7. The music attracted large crowds to the concert in Chicago Illinois.

14 Cove Creek

Latara Tennessee

August 16 1987

Dear Aunt Hattie

Thanks for such a practical, fun gift. Boards nails hinges a hammer and plans for a birdhouse—what more could anyone ask for?

Your niece

Toni

You should have added 19 commas and circled nine animal names.
NOW, on the back of this paper, write a sentence to illustrate each rule above.

Bonus Box: Think of a category, such as plants, foods, or colors. Write five sentences in which names of items in this category are hidden. Let a classmate find your hidden words.

 Best of THE MAILBOX • INTERMEDIATE • ©The Education Center, Inc. • Sue Nations, Sylva, NC   Keys pp. 189-191

Name ______________________________ Punctuation: using commas and semicolons

Decisions, Decisions

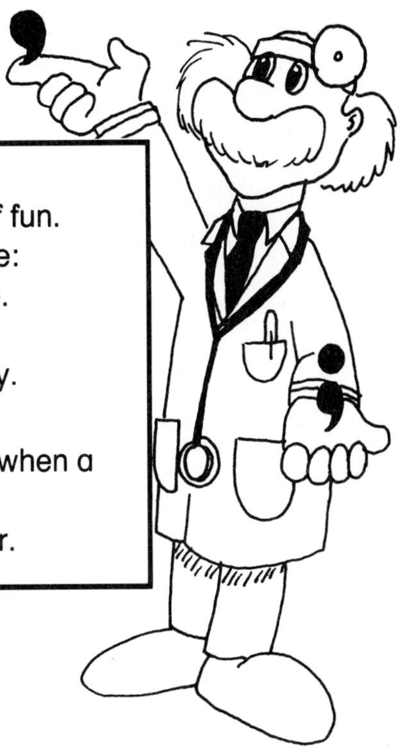

How do you know when to use a comma or a semicolon?

- Use a comma:
  1. to set off an interrupting phrase: Reading, I believe, is lots of fun.
  2. to set off an introductory clause from the rest of the sentence:
     While Mary read her book, Nathan listened to the radio.
  3. to separate adjectives that are not joined by a conjunction:
     Her proud, smiling father watched the awards ceremony.
- Use a semicolon:
  4. between the independent clauses of a compound sentence when a conjunction is not used:
     The biggest snow came in April; it was unusual weather.

Directions: Add commas or semicolons to the sentences.
Color in the circle under the correct column.

Comma	Semicolon	
(N)	(B)	1. We used a net to land the huge flopping fish.
(R)	(C)	2. After the storm had passed workers cleared the roads.
(D)	(G)	3. Many friends gathered at Tom's house it was a party.
(E)	(H)	4. The program which started at 7:00 lasted two hours.
(I)	(F)	5. Jack knows how to handle applause he is often in the winner's circle.
(A)	(T)	6. Maureen I think decided to go to Six Flags.
(K)	(J)	7. A squatty frog which eats tons of insects has lived under our porch for years.
(S)	(L)	8. Before you leave school make sure you're ready for the play.
(B)	(Z)	9. Mother likes to go to the mountains Dad prefers the beach.
(E)	(M)	10. Piles of lovely colorful gifts were on the table.

Unscramble the letters in the comma column to find the name of the most mysterious shoe: ___ ___ ___ ___ ___ ___ ___

Bonus Box: Number the back of this sheet 1-10. Write the number of the rule you used to correct each sentence above.

Planning for Successful Parent Conferences

Planning ahead for parent conferences can help you avoid tense moments and prevent conference jitters. Try these teacher-tested tips to establish a friendly atmosphere and positive attitudes.

- The day before conferences, my students make cookies. I put these out with a fresh pot of coffee, tea, or hot cocoa to welcome parents.

  Linda Crissman
  Gratis, OH

- I display photographs of my students taken during a Halloween party or other event to provide enjoyment for parents who are waiting to meet the teacher. I move my class easel into the hall, mount the photos, and add a title.

  Coreen Stamper
  Cleveland, OH

- To prepare for teacher conference day, keep an index card for each child in your classroom. Jot down the positive things about each child or behavioral incidents during the course of the year. Too many times we forget to mention these important little things to parents.

  Lila Lynne
  Williston, ND

- To relieve students' anxiety about conference time, discuss the purposes of the conferences with them before they are scheduled. Students may decide that they would like to participate in the conferences too, if agreeable with parents. Have students provide items they would like the teacher to share with their parents. Input from the student can help parents and the teacher understand the child's feelings about the areas to be covered and provides a more-relaxed atmosphere.

  Jewel Harmon
  Mountain City, TN

- Prior to conference time, send home a survey for each parent to complete and return at the conference. This helps parents examine their child's education and prepare for the conference. (Some sample questions might be: What do you feel is your child's best subject? What do you think is your child's weakest subject? How does your child feel about school?) Add questions to the survey that pertain to your class.

  Sharleen Berg
  Red Wing, MN

- Try to end each conference on an optimistic note. Parents should leave with a hopeful feeling. Positive attitudes and your suggestions can help parents help their children.

  Deborah Gardner
  Trenton, NJ

- Move from behind the desk to ease parent tension. Arrange the teacher's chair and parents' chairs in a semicircle. If possible, provide adult-size chairs. Establish a comfortable room temperature as well as a comfortable climate for communication.

  Carla A. Jones
  Cleburne, TX

- Before my first conference begins, I make sure I have a notepad and several sharpened pencils on the conference table. If a question comes up during the conference, I can jot it down and get back to the parents at a later date. Parents can write down things they want to remember or comments they want to share with their children.

Pamela Myhowich
Auburn, WA

- To save time for parents and avoid scheduling problems for teachers, make a list of parents who have two or more children in the same school. With other teachers, plan consecutive times for these parents to come in to school. Extra trips for parents can be avoided.

Rose Rasmussen
Mountain City, TN

- I have children make nametags for parents. Each child writes his name and his parent's name on the nametag. I tape the nametags to the classroom door. When the parents arrive, they take their nametags off the door and wear them.

Sr. Margaret Ann Wooden
Martinsburg, WV

- Be specific! Prepare for the conference by providing a folder of each child's work which has been selected specifically to support comments you plan to make. This statement, for example, is too vague: "Bill needs to work on math." A better way to clarify it for parents would be: "Bill is having difficulty in adding two-digit numbers with regrouping, as you can see." Include good work too!

Paula K. Holdren
Prospect, KY

- To prepare for parent conferences, our staff holds a group meeting where we role-play various situations which may arise. Teachers select situations (late parent, angry parent, parent who gets off the topic) and demonstrate how they would handle them. Colleagues learn from the responses of others and evaluate the ways they handled the situations. This helps us conduct good, productive conferences.

Paula K. Holdren

- To keep things running smoothly, I put up a sign that says "Knock when it's your conference time." I post a list of parents and times on my door. This helps me keep on schedule by drawing long-winded conferences to a close. Prompt arrivals do not end up waiting because the previous person was late. Having this reminder takes the burden off me.

Paula K. Holdren

- Conferences should not be dominated by the teacher. There should be give-and-take. To encourage parents to talk freely, I ask them to express their concerns or ask their questions first. I follow up with what I have learned about their child and give positive feedback whenever I can. Parents also like to hear what they are doing right!

Frances V. Lawrence
Chevy Chase, MD

- It's important to find out how kids are feeling about themselves and their work. Before conferences each year, I have my students make their own "report cards." On the cards, they write their names, the areas they think they are doing well in, and the areas in which they are having difficulty. I present these cards to the parents during conferences. We compare each child's view of himself with the teacher's and parents' perceptions.

Pamela Myhowich

- Ask the parent what the child says at home about school. What does he or she like/dislike? Ask the parent to name his child's strengths and weaknesses as the parent sees them. Ask what kinds of discipline or rewards work best with the child. By getting a picture of the child at home, the teacher is better able to help the child achieve in school.

Darce Easton
Hagerstown, MD

- I provide punch and a plate of cookies during conferences. The parents and children enjoy the treat, and it makes for a more relaxed atmosphere.

Sr. Margaret Ann Wooden

Ghosts And Ghouls And Creatures That Go Bump In The Night

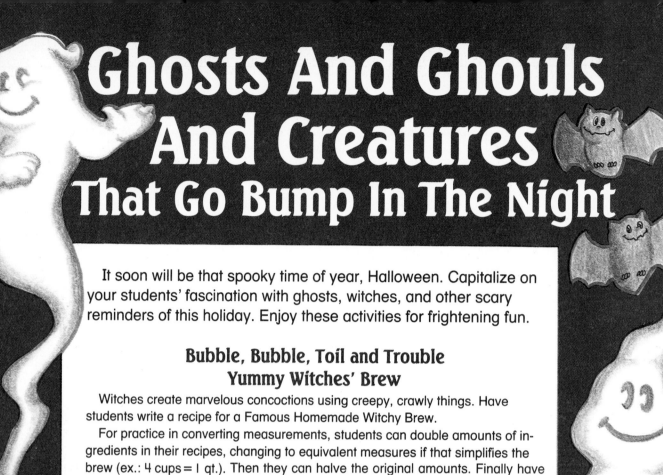

It soon will be that spooky time of year, Halloween. Capitalize on your students' fascination with ghosts, witches, and other scary reminders of this holiday. Enjoy these activities for frightening fun.

Bubble, Bubble, Toil and Trouble
Yummy Witches' Brew

Witches create marvelous concoctions using creepy, crawly things. Have students write a recipe for a Famous Homemade Witchy Brew.

For practice in converting measurements, students can double amounts of ingredients in their recipes, changing to equivalent measures if that simplifies the brew (ex.: 4 cups = 1 qt.). Then they can halve the original amounts. Finally have students convert the recipe to metric measurements.

Well-known Haunted Hangouts

There are a number of places commonly believed to be haunted. Each student chooses a place such as a castle, a haunted house, an old hotel, or the White House. He writes a descriptive story about ways that he'd haunt it if he were a ghost, then adds an illustration to haunt readers.

The Ghost Of A Famous Person

Legend has it that some famous people came back to haunt people or places with which they were familiar. Each student chooses a famous, deceased person whose ghost he would like to meet. Who would it be? Where would they meet? The student writes the conversation that they might have and gives reasons for choosing that person.

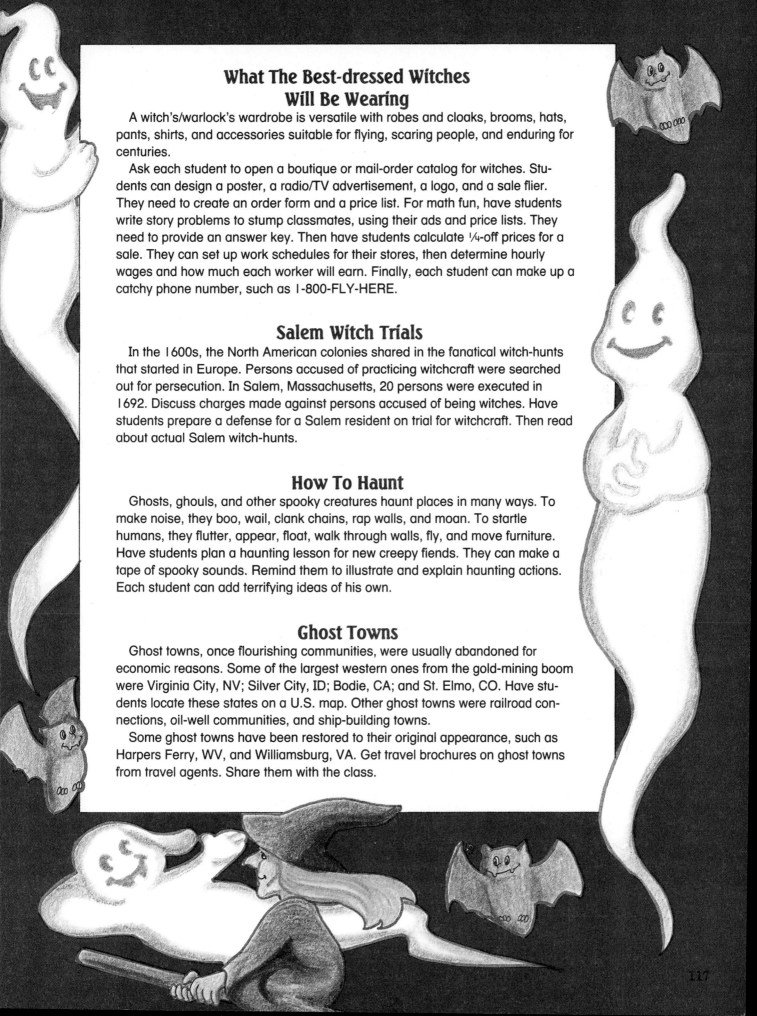

What The Best-dressed Witches
Will Be Wearing

A witch's/warlock's wardrobe is versatile with robes and cloaks, brooms, hats, pants, shirts, and accessories suitable for flying, scaring people, and enduring for centuries.

Ask each student to open a boutique or mail-order catalog for witches. Students can design a poster, a radio/TV advertisement, a logo, and a sale flier. They need to create an order form and a price list. For math fun, have students write story problems to stump classmates, using their ads and price lists. They need to provide an answer key. Then have students calculate ¼-off prices for a sale. They can set up work schedules for their stores, then determine hourly wages and how much each worker will earn. Finally, each student can make up a catchy phone number, such as 1-800-FLY-HERE.

Salem Witch Trials

In the 1600s, the North American colonies shared in the fanatical witch-hunts that started in Europe. Persons accused of practicing witchcraft were searched out for persecution. In Salem, Massachusetts, 20 persons were executed in 1692. Discuss charges made against persons accused of being witches. Have students prepare a defense for a Salem resident on trial for witchcraft. Then read about actual Salem witch-hunts.

How To Haunt

Ghosts, ghouls, and other spooky creatures haunt places in many ways. To make noise, they boo, wail, clank chains, rap walls, and moan. To startle humans, they flutter, appear, float, walk through walls, fly, and move furniture. Have students plan a haunting lesson for new creepy fiends. They can make a tape of spooky sounds. Remind them to illustrate and explain haunting actions. Each student can add terrifying ideas of his own.

Ghost Towns

Ghost towns, once flourishing communities, were usually abandoned for economic reasons. Some of the largest western ones from the gold-mining boom were Virginia City, NV; Silver City, ID; Bodie, CA; and St. Elmo, CO. Have students locate these states on a U.S. map. Other ghost towns were railroad connections, oil-well communities, and ship-building towns.

Some ghost towns have been restored to their original appearance, such as Harpers Ferry, WV, and Williamsburg, VA. Get travel brochures on ghost towns from travel agents. Share them with the class.

TURKEY TALK

Give your classroom the flavor of fall with a little turkey talk! Provide these activities for students to do in their free time or assign them as class projects.

- Talk turkey! Discover how this bird was named by the Pilgrims. Find out how it almost became our national symbol. Write a paragraph to convince your friends that the turkey should or should not be our national bird.

- What are turkey ranches? What state produces the most turkeys? What do we call male turkeys? females? young turkeys? Draw a turkey. Label these parts: spurs, wattle, caruncles.

- Create a TV commercial telling the advantages of eating turkey. How many different recipes can you find for turkey? List them.

- "Carve" a turkey! Write your spelling words on a turkey worksheet. Mount the worksheet on poster board. Cut the turkey into puzzle pieces for a classmate to assemble.

- Examine a turkey feather. Draw and label the vane, rachis, down, barbs, and quill. Tell why birds have feathers. What is molting? What uses did Native Americans have for feathers? How many uses for turkey feathers can you think of?

- Create a colonial Thanksgiving feast. This is not only a lesson in cooking but also a history lesson. The recipes of the colonial period reflect the times and the European cultures that came together in America. The Pilgrims and early pioneers had to adapt their favorite recipes to those ingredients available. For recipes and fascinating historical background, check out *Slumps, Grunts, and Snickerdoodles, What Colonial America Ate and Why* by Lila Perl (Houghton Mifflin, 1975). Bring in one colonial food, and tell how and why it was prepared long ago.

- Demonstrate how the Pilgrims dipped candles, made paper, dried fruits, or made butter.

- Learn a Thanksgiving hymn or recite a poem for choral speaking.

- Make a Thanksgiving Day coaster. Collect samples of dried flowers, seedpods, nuts, and weeds from along roadsides. Cover a work area with newspaper. Arrange bits and pieces of flora on a lid from a margarine tub. Cover carefully with a layer of clear Modge Podge™. Allow to harden overnight on a flat surface.

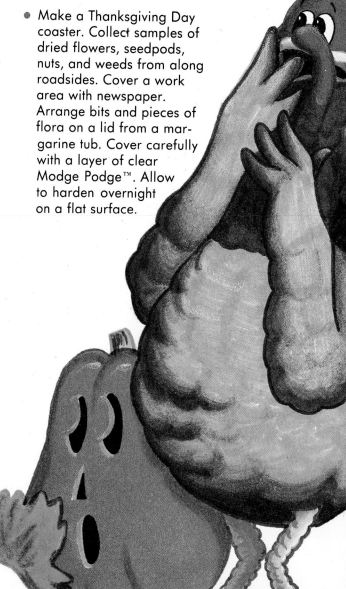

Out Space into Space

It's time to launch an enthusiasm for science! What better unit than space travel? Fascinate your students with the wonders of space while you provide practice in language arts, research skills, and more! See the related reproducible on page 121.

Book Boosters

Rockets are often made up of separate parts called *stages* or *boosters*. When the fuel in a booster is used up, the booster is dropped, or jettisoned. Encourage wide reading interests with a multistage bulletin board. Duplicate copies of the rocket on page 121. Each student writes his name at the top and a book category in each stage. Staple rockets to the board. When a student reads a book in stage one's category, he cuts that stage off the rocket. When all three stages are jettisoned, reward the student with a bookmark or special treat.

nar Superstitions

an finally stepped foot on the moon on 20, 1969. For years many people believed our moon could bring good or ill luck. De-t your students with these silly supersti-s. Then have them write stories explaining they think the myths got started.

Silver coins jingling in your pocket during a new moon bring good luck.
A new moon is the best time to: get a haircut, take a trip, make a wish, cut your fingernails, find a sweetheart.
To get rid of a wart, rub your hand over it dur-ing a new moon.
It's bad luck to see a woman combing her hair in the light of the moon.
It's bad luck to plant seeds during a full moon.
Glimpsing the moon over your left shoulder is bad luck.
If you see the new moon reflected in a well, you'll have bad luck.
If you sleep with moonlight on your face, you'll go crazy.
Moonlight dulls razors.

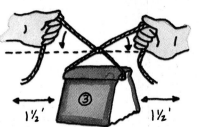

Gravity's Grip

The sun, moon, and all the planets have gravity, but it is the earth's gravity that astronauts must beat before they can escape into space. Demonstrate gravity's grip with this experiment:

1. Open a heavy book and place it in the center of a five-foot length of cord, facedown.
2. Tie a knot in the cord at the book's spine.

3. Take one end of the cord in each hand at least 1½ feet away from the book and pull. Try to bring the cord into a perfectly horizontal position with the knot in the center.

It can't be done! Gravity's grip on the book is too strong. Explain that the only way man has found to escape gravity is with speed. Rockets must leave earth fast enough to escape before gravity can pull the rocket back.

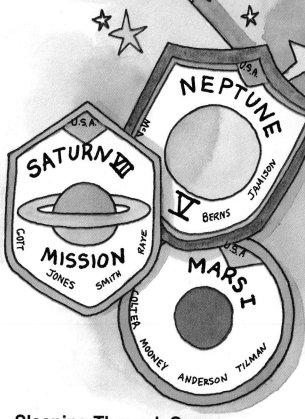

What's Your Mission?

Every space mission sets out with certain objectives. For example, the goal of Project Apollo's mission was to land American explorers on the moon, bring them back safely to earth, and establish new technology. Divide your class into eight mission teams, one to research each planet (excluding earth). After researching, have each group decide on three or four objectives for an imaginary trip to their planet. What questions would they like their mission to answer? What would they hope to discover? Discuss objectives in class as a way to share group research.

Planetary Patches

Incorporate a fun art activity into "What's Your Mission?" NASA develops a uniform patch for each mission with a special design and the last names of the astronauts. Have each group design their own large mission patch on butcher paper. Provide paint, crayons, or chalk for coloring. Display finished patches on a "Planetary Patches" bulletin board.

Space Museum

Turn your classroom into a space history museum. Assign groups of two to three students a famous space personality to research. With their findings, students create original museum displays using posters, tapes, models, drawings, and other media. When all displays are completed, organize them in your room and hold an Open House. Invite other classes to come meet these famous men and women of space.

Robert Goddard	Jules Verne	H.G. Wells
John Glenn	Neil Armstrong	Yuri Gagarin
Alan B. Shepard, Jr.	Valentina V. Tereshkova	Virgil I. Grissom
Sally Ride		Guion Bluford

Sleeping Through Space

In planning long-distance flights, scientists are experimenting with "frozen sleep" which is similar to hibernation. By the time astronauts would awake, they would be closer to their destination. What would it be like to wake up after ten years of space sleep? For a fun free-time activity, post a large piece of paper labeled with the following question: "What would be the first question you would ask Mission Control when you awoke after ten years of sleep?" Let children write their questions on the poster during spare time. The results should be interesting!

Book Boosters

Cut out the rocket.
Write a book category
in each stage.

(Use with activity
on page 119.)

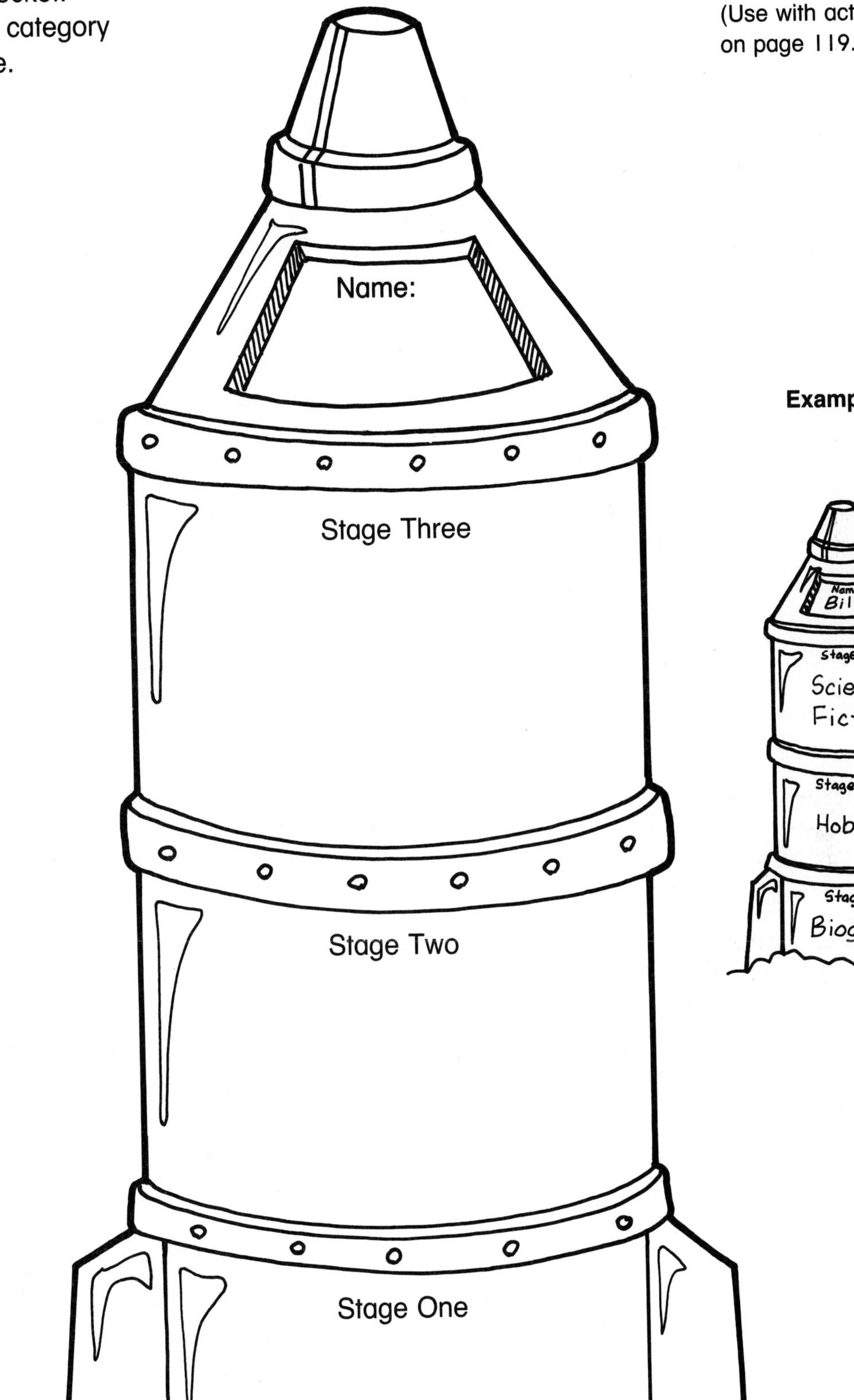

Name:

Stage Three

Stage Two

Stage One

Example

Name:
Billy

Stage Three
Science
Fiction

Stage Two
Hobbies

Stage One
Biography

Joy To The World

A Look At International December Holidays

Broaden your students' holiday horizons with these activities from December celebrations around the world. Add to the international flavor by asking children to share holiday traditions their parents and grandparents may have brought from other countries. Have a globe-trotting Christmas this year!

Africa

Kwanza is an African harvest festival celebrated on the last seven days of the year. Each day commemorates a different "food for life": unity, determination, responsibility, economy, purpose, creativity, and faith. Families celebrate by lighting symbolic candles during each night of the festival and decorate their homes with banners of red, green, and black. Observe Kwanza in your classroom by having students exchange traditional gift necklaces made from red, green, and black painted macaroni. Drape Kwanza chains labeled with the seven foods for life around your room.

Belgium

A child in Belgium doesn't want to be the last one out of bed on St. Sylvester's Day, December 31! The sleepyhead of the family earns the title "Sylvester" and must pay a fine to brothers and sisters. Find the Sylvesters in your room with this math activity. Divide students into small groups of five or six, and provide each group with graph paper. Have students prepare a bar graph showing the wake-up time for each group member. Compare all groups' results. Decide on funny rewards and penalties for the early birds, the average risers, and the Sylvesters.

Sweden

Celebrate the sun with Swedish families on St. Lucia's Day, December 13. On this day, a daughter, wearing a white robe and a crown of lighted candles, walks from room to room waking her family. A traditional breakfast of coffee and *lussekatter,* a sweet saffron-flavored bread, is served. Try this easy version of lussekatter for independent small-group cooking. You'll need two cans of refrigerated breakfast rolls with icing, two cookie sheets, and some small candles.

1. Pop open both cans of refrigerated rolls.
2. On a large cookie sheet, place eight of the rolls in a circle so that the rolls touch.
3. Form a second circle, using six rolls, on another cookie sheet.
4. Bake according to the directions on the can.
5. When done, place the smaller circle on top of the large one, and drizzle icing over both.
6. Decorate with candles and garnishes for an easy St. Lucia's crown that tastes delicious!

India

Divali, the Indian festival of lights, is observed each year in December. The three-day celebration honors *Lakshmi*, the goddess of good luck and prosperity. Families scrub their homes until they're spotless, and prepare *diya* lamps by placing wicks in small bowls filled with oil. On the last night of the celebration, children float their diya lamps across the river. If the light burns until a lamp floats out of view, the family will have good luck. This diya lamp bulletin board will send your students off with good wishes for the year ahead. Cut out a lamp for each child, with a separate piece to represent a flame. On the back of each flame write a personal message. Post the lamps and the flames, message side to the bulletin board. Each day, while students are out of the room, remove three or four flames and place them in students' desks. Children look forward to reading their personal notes as well as watching to see which students have received their wishes.

Ireland

On December 26, Wren Day, the Irish tell an old story. When the birds gathered to choose a king, they decided that the bird who flew the highest would be crowned. The sly wren hid on the eagle's back and remained there until the eagle was at the peak of his flight. The wren then flew out, higher even than the mighty eagle. Irish children carry a stuffed wren from house to house as they carol, earning a few coins for their songs. Remember the day by making eagle and wren mascots out of brown grocery bags stuffed with newspaper and decorated with cut-out wings and feathers. Play favorite skill games today, but give them a King Wren twist: lowest card wins in a game of War, the child with the smallest number of matches wins in Concentration, last one to reach the end of a trail game is the winner.

Mexico

For nine nights in December, Mexican children search for shelter just as Mary and Joseph did in Bethlehem. This celebration, beginning on December 13, is known as the *Posadas*, for "inn or lodging house." Carrying paper lanterns on long poles, the Posada participants parade down streets lit with fireworks, ending up at someone's home for treats to eat. Use the steps below to make Posada lanterns for your room out of construction paper or art foil.

1. Fold rectangle in half lengthwise.
2. Make an outward fold on each side.
3. Cut slits about ¼" apart from center fold up to outward fold lines.
4. Open up the rectangle and roll it into a cylinder. Fasten edges with paste.
5. Add a handle and hang!

Claudia Vurnakes
Greensboro, NC

123

Day of the Dinosaur

Looking for a great way to breathe some life into your midwinter curriculum? Invite some "terrible lizards" into your classroom for a variety of basic skills activities.

A, B, C, D-inosaur

Here's a list for dinosaur enthusiasts—a beast for every letter of the alphabet! Enhance research skills by assigning one dinosaur to each student to investigate. Have students summarize their findings. Use the list for alphabetizing or handwriting practice, too.

Ankylosaurus (ang-KILE-uh-sawr-us)
Brachiosaurus (BRAK-ee-uh-sawr-us)
Corythosaurus (ko-RITH-uh-sawr-us)
Diplodocus (dih-PLOD-uh-kus)
Edmontosaurus (ed-MON-tuh-sawr-us)
Fabrosaurus (FAB-ruh-sawr-us)
Gorgosaurus (GOR-guh-sawr-us)
Hypsilophodon (hip-sih-LO-fuh-don)
Iguanodon (ig-WAN-oh-don)
Jaxartosaurus (jax-AR-tuh-sawr-us)
Kentrosaurus (KEN-truh-sawr-us)
Lambeosaurus (LAM-be-uh-sawr-us)
Megalosaurus (MEG-uh-lo-sawr-us)

Nodosaurus (no-doe-SAWR-us)
Ornitholestes (or-nith-o-LES-teez)
Protoceratops (pro-toe-SAIR-uh-tops)
Quetzalcoatlus (ket-sol-ko-AT-lus)
Rhamphorhyncus (ram-fo-RINK-us)
Stegosaurus (STEG-uh-sawr-us)
Tarbosaurus (TAR-bo-sawr-us)
Ultrasaurus (UL-truh-sawr-us)
Velociraptor (veh-loss-ih-RAP-tor)
Wuerhosaurus (WER-ho-sawr-us)
Xiphactinus (zi-FAK-tuh-nus)
Yaleosaurus (YALE-ee-o-sawr-us)
Zigongosaurus (sih-GON-guh-sawr-us)

Take A Bronto Break

Here's a quick and easy bulletin board to fill with creative student work. Enlarge the brontosaurus pattern on page 126. Laminate and post on a bulletin board. Use a wipe-off marker to write a task on the dinosaur. Students complete the task during free time. Staple their completed work to the board. Wipe clean and change the assignment after several days.

List 10 ways to catch a Tyrannosaurus Rex.
Draw a picture of a dinosaur department store.
Write an advertisement for a baby-sitter for your pet Brontosaurus.
Write directions for giving a Stegosaurus a bath.
Design a cover for the book *Dinosaur Nursery Rhymes*.
Choose a dinosaur. Describe its habitat and means of protection.
Tell why you think the dinosaurs disappeared. Give at least three reasons for your opinion.

Fossil Find

Bone up on map skills with this latitude and longitude activity. Use the pattern on page 126 to make ten cut-out bones. Number and label each with a latitude and longitude direction. Post on a bulletin board around a world map. During free time, students use the map to identify the country and continent of each fossil bone. Share correct answers at the end of the week.

Bones:
1. 25° N and 30° E (Egypt, Africa)
2. 25° S and 135° E (Australia)
3. 16° N and 100° E (Thailand, Asia)
4. 60° N and 110° W (Canada, North America)
5. 22° N and 102° W (Mexico, North America)
6. 15° S and 50° W (Brazil, South America)
7. 40° N and 5° W (Spain, Europe)
8. 40° N and 100° E (China, Asia)
9. 20° N and 80° E (India, Asia)
10. 80° S and 20° W (Antarctica)

Terrible T. Rex Game

Students will enjoy reviewing any unit or skill with the help of this game. Duplicate 20 to 30 bones using the pattern on page 126. Label each bone with the name of a dinosaur (see "A, B, C, D-inosaur" on page 124). Label four bones with "Terrible T. Rex." Place cutouts in a box.

To play, divide the class into two teams. In turn, ask a player a question. If answered correctly, the player pulls a bone from the box. The team with the most bones at the end of the game wins. If a player draws a "Terrible T. Rex" cutout, his team loses one of their bones.

Land Of The Giants

Turn your classroom into the "Land of the Giants" with a 3-D art project. Divide the class into groups of two to three students each. For each group, staple together two large sheets of butcher paper along the edges. Students draw and cut out the outline of their favorite dinosaur. After painting the front and back of their dinosaur, students staple along the edge, leaving a small opening for stuffing. Stuff with newspaper, scrap fabric, or plastic bags, and finish stapling. Then bring your camera and take "family portraits" of the creatures and their creators to place in your class scrapbook.

The Long And Short Of It

Provide important math practice while you study the prehistoric past. Post the chart of dinosaur lengths. Write a "Prehistoric Problem of the Day" on the board. Students use the information on the chart to solve the problem. Let students submit their original problems for consideration also.

Head outside on a sunny day with meter sticks and tape measures to mark off the length of each dinosaur. Students will be amazed at the size of these ancient beasts.

Dinosaur Lengths	
Triceratops	10 meters
Stegosaurus	6 meters
Diplodocus	29 meters
Ankylosaurus	7 meters
Dimetrodon	3 meters
Trachodon	13 meters
Protoceratops	2 meters
Styracosaurus	5 meters
Tyrannosaurus	15 meters

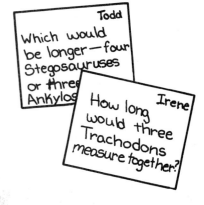

Todd
Which would be longer—four Stegosauruses or three Ankylos

Irene
How long would three Trachodons measure together?

Patterns

See the activities for
using these patterns
on pages 124 and 125.

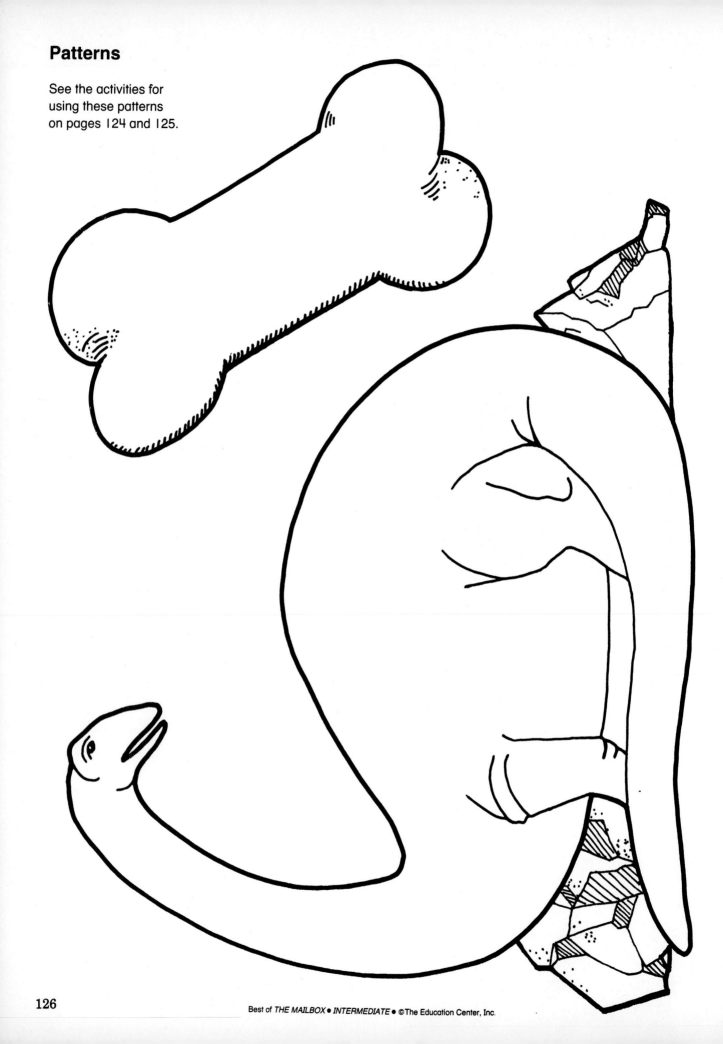

★ ★

Spotlight Your State

Get acquainted with your own home state with a variety of activities that your students can help to make.

Know Your State

Involve your students in constructing this Pocket Pal center. Draw an outline of your state on the back of a string-tie envelope. Use colorful sticky dots for the trail. Have each student make up two or three review questions about your state. After checking their work, have students write each question on the front of a cut-out card and the answer on the back. Store the cards in the envelope with a coin and markers. You and your students can add additional cards as new material is covered.

Melissa Matusevich
Blacksburg, VA

Student Directions:
1. In turn, draw a card and give the answer. Turn the card over to check.
2. If correct, flip a coin and move: Heads: 2 spaces. Tails: 1 space.
3. If incorrect, do not flip the coin.
4. First to FINISH wins.

What's In a Name?

Every state has a nickname with an origin all its own. After discussing your state nickname, ask each student to create a new nickname, one which captures an important quality of your state. Each student writes a paragraph giving the nickname and the reasons for choosing it. After sharing paragraphs, have students use tagboard strips to design original bumper stickers displaying the new nicknames.

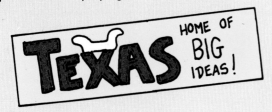

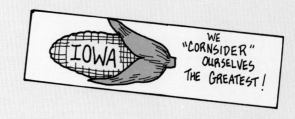

Map Match-Up

Magnetic tape makes this state geography poster special. Trace an outline of your state on poster board. Number important places. Attach a small piece of magnetic tape beside each number. Label cut-out stars with matching place names. Place magnetic tape on the back of each star. Store stars and an answer key in a pocket attached to the back of the poster.

Melissa Matusevich

Footsteps of History

Enlist student aid to prepare a state history center. Place a box filled with markers and 10-20 large cut-out footprints at your social studies center. During free time, students take a footprint and label it with an important event in your state's history. When all footprints are labeled, individual students place them in order on the floor. Be sure to number-code the backs of the footprints for self-checking.

Melissa Matusevich

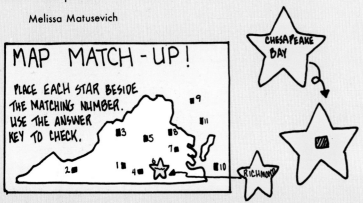

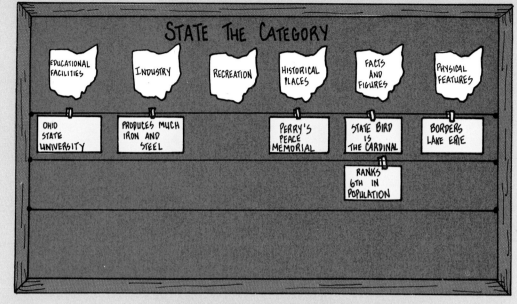

State the Category

Teamwork makes this bulletin board a snap to complete. Label several cut-outs of your state with categories and place on a bulletin board. String several clotheslines across the board. Place a folder of blank cut-out cards near the board. Students label cards with places or facts about your state. Then they clip cards under the correct categories on the board. Use for a visual review of your state study, along with categorization practice.

Melissa Matusevich
Blacksburg, VA

Now and Then

Take a step back in time with this chart activity. Post the list of topics, and give each child a copy of the blank chart shown. Have each student fill in the first column with any five topics. Students then read about your state's early settlers in resource books and complete the chart. Discuss their findings to compare the settler's life to life now.

Topics
Food
Clothing
Recreation
Religion
Education
Architecture
Agriculture
Government
Medicine
Transportation

State Scavengers

Explore your state without leaving your classroom holding a scavenger hunt. Obtain road maps from your State Transportation Department. Give each pair students a map and a list of places and landmarks in your state. Students locate each place on the map and list the county in which it is found. The team locating the most items on their list wins.

The Great Divide

Get your students thinking about your state's resources, geography, population and other features with a hypothetical situation: Your state has decided to divide into two separate states. Where would you want to divide the state? Why? What would you call the new states? What would be the advantages/disadvantages of living in either of the new states? Discuss answers in small groups, then with everyone together.

Let your students do the teaching with these group activities. Be sure to set aside time to share and evaluate group projects.

Giant State Booklet

Divide into groups of three to four students each, and give each group one of the topics listed below. Provide plenty of resource books. Also give each group a large state shape cut from butcher paper. After researching their topics, groups write their findings on their cut out. Students may use poetry, paragraphs, lists, drawings or any other method to present their information. Bind the cutouts in a giant booklet to display in the school lobby or library.

TOPICS
Government
Industry
Recreation/Tourism
Education
Climate
Vegetation
Bodies of Water
Minerals
Major Cities

State Tours, Inc.

All states encourage tourism to boost their local economies. Learn about your state's resources and recreational opportunities by having groups design large travel brochures. The brochures should advertise reasons to visit your state, including tourist attractions, climate, natural resources, major cities and recreational facilities. Those groups with true entrepreneurial spirit may also want to design bumper stickers, billboards, T-shirts, or television commercials to encourage tourism.

Personality Plus

Invite colorful characters from your state's history to your classroom. Assign each group of two to three students a famous state personality from the past to research. Each group writes a short biography of their person and records it on a cassette tape. Students draw their person on the back of a large paper plate and staple half of another plate behind it to form a pocket. Store the tape in the pocket and place at a listening center.

Who Am I?

Follow up Personality Plus with a famous people file folder. Attach pockets labeled with the names of the Personality Plus people to the inside of a file folder. Have each group label five to eight cards with facts about their person. Code the backs of the cards for self-checking, and store in a pocket attached to the back of the folder.

Melissa Matusevich
Blacksburg, VA

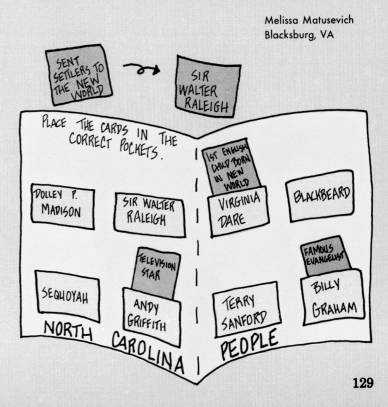

The Magic Of Hot-Air Ballooning

Raise your class spirits aloft with a colorful, high-flying special unit on balloons. Soar through these activities for math, research, language arts, management, and more. See the accompanying worksheet and **pattern on pages 132 and 133.**

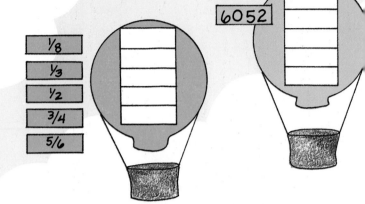

Whatever Goes Up And Up And Up...

Hot-air balloons are only one of the things that can fly. List everything that you can think of that flies. Can you list 25, 50, 75, . . .?

butterfly
witch
jet
hang glider
flying squirrel
airplane
bat (a mammal)
seeds
blimp
rocket
insects
helium balloon
Mary Poppins
ghost
kite
moth
Superman

Up, Up, And Away

Display hot-air balloons in several colors with spaces for five sequencing cards in the center of each. (See the pattern on page 133.) Make five number cards in a corresponding color for each balloon. Students get to be high risers by correctly sequencing each set of numbers. Vary with card sets for sequencing fractions, decimals, measures of length, or groups of coins.

Shirley Liby
Muncie, IN

Two Hundred Years Of Ballooning

Ballooning is an activity that has been around for many years. Through resea with this file folder, students will recognize and appreciate accomplishments in t wild blue yonder of hot-air ballooning.

Use encyclopedias and other reference sources to discover the history of balloon flight. Find out inventors, the years of their inventions, and specific accomplishments.

Share what you discover with the class via a timeline, pictures, a mobile, a report, or another means.

A few facts to get you started!

June 5, 1783—Coinventor brothers made first balloon flight: Joseph an Jacques Montgolfier—Annonay, France.

June 4, 1784—First woman in history to fly in free balloon: Marie Thible—Lyons, France.

August 17, 1978—First balloon crossing of Atlantic Ocean (3,200 miles): Americans—Max Anderson Ben Arbruzzo, Larry New (from Albuquerque, NM) in "Double Eagl II."

Fly With Your Imagination

Pretend that you are in the basket, *gondola*, of a balloon floating high above the patchwork of fields far below. Write a poem about your flight, using a poetry style of your choice. (See the open worksheet on page 132.) Illustrate. Then add it to the book of balloon poems by the class.

Extension: Combine oral reading of these poems with student-selected music and background posters, murals, or slides for a class audiovisual interpretation of ballooning.

A Reason To Fly

There are many purposes for flying hot-air balloons. Some of these are for commercial, hobby, racing, travel, and scientific reasons. Use library reference books to discover more about these reasons for ballooning. Head your paper with a column for each category. List examples of flight that fall in that category. Use words, phrases, pictures, advertisements, etc. Add any other categories that you find. Display.

Ballooning				
Commercial	Hobby	Racing	Travel	Scientific
to advertise company names or products		trying to land closest to given target	honeymoon	weather

Be On "Cloud 9"

These clouds labeled from Cloud One to Nine are a perfect way to keep track of student progress through multiplication tables. Student names are written on the correct cloud according to the level of facts mastered. Those on Cloud 9 may earn a sticker or prize. Cotton may be used for a 3-D effect.

Merleen Ivey
Jackson, MS

Balloons In Our Lives

Make a classroom display using cutouts of hot-air balloons from available sources, such as magazines, newspapers, etc. Encourage students to bring in more pictures to expand the display.

Then have students design pictures of their own hot-air balloons. Display these also.

Sandra Horst
Bismarck, ND

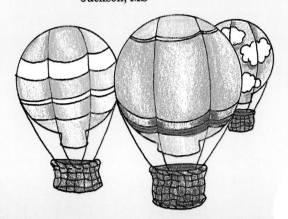

Lofty Thoughts

Note To Teacher: Use for creative writing, balloon activities, spelling tests, writing letters, etc.

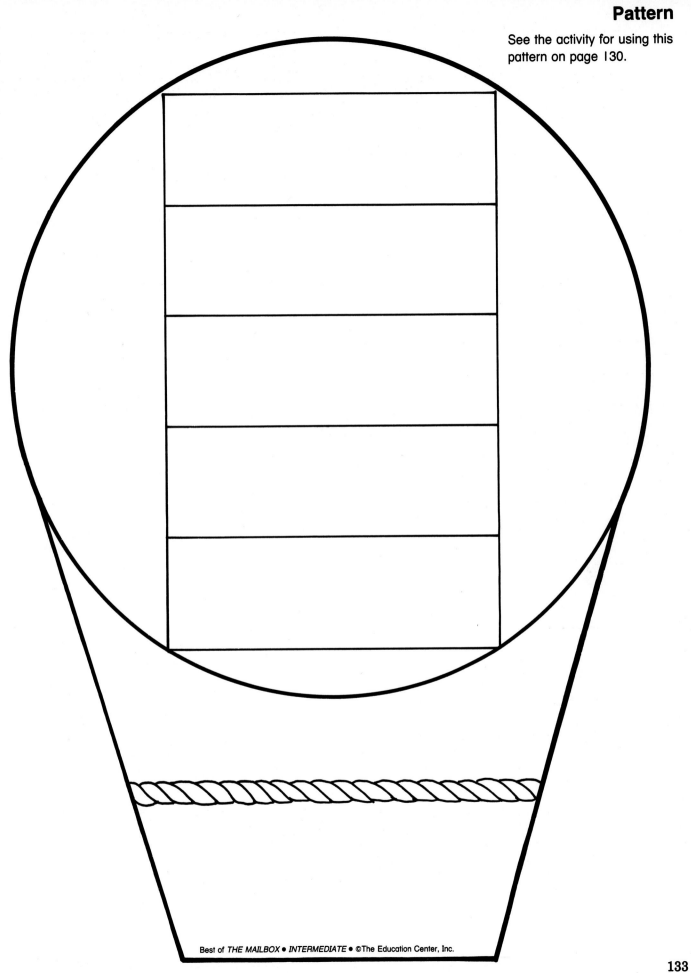

Mexico

Say "Olé" to a fact-finding tour of our neighbor to the south, Mexico. Invite your students to discover the magic of Mexico with these activities. See accompanying worksheets and pattern on pages 136–138.

Rebecca G. Simpson
Winston-Salem, NC

Piece-by-Piece

Let your students be the experts with a group research project. Divide students into several groups and assign a topic below to each. Cut a large piece of butcher paper into jigsaw puzzle pieces and give each group a piece, labeled with their topic. Have students research their topic and place the information on their puzzle piece, using pictures, captions, poetry, etc. After each group shares their information with the class, reassemble the puzzle on a bulletin board for a giant study aid that all can enjoy.

Land and Climate of Mexico
Mexican City Life
Mexican Village Life
History of Mexico

Mexican Food
Mexican Clothing
Mexican Government
Mexican Holidays

Parrot Collage

Parrots are particularly loved as pets in Mexico. For a colorful collage project, have students draw a large parrot on construction paper using a **permanent** marker. Tear brightly colored tissue paper into small pieces. Dilute white glue with water. Students "color" their parrots by placing a piece of colored tissue paper on the pet and brushing over it with a paintbrush dipped in glue (the glue will dry clear).

Rest-in-Peace, Mexican-Style

One of the favorite holidays of Mexican children is the Day of the Dead on November 2. Families honor dead relatives by flocking to cemeteries with flowers and having merry picnics by the graves. Mexicans also write humorous obituaries for living persons, usually in verse. Have students discuss the format of newspaper obituaries, then write a humorous obituary for themselves, a friend, or a favorite television personality. After proofreading, students copy their obituary onto a cut-out gravestone. Bind gravestones into a class book or post on a bulletin board.

Mexican Hall Of Fame

Montezuma

Santa Anna

Miguel Hidalgo

Benito Juárez

↑ Fold ↑

Turn a large bulletin board into a museum of Mexico's famous personalities. Cut out several large sombreros as shown. (See the pattern on page 138.) Fold up along the dotted line and staple to form a pocket. Label each sombrero with the name of a famous Mexican. Provide a pocket and small cards. Students write a fact about a person on a card and insert it in the appropriate pocket. Later remove the cards and have students try to match the cards to the correct sombrero.

The Legend Of Popo and Izta

Two snow-capped volcanoes, Iztaccihuatl and Popocatepetl, overlook Mexico City. Iztaccihuatl, or Izta for short, is shaped like a woman lying on her back. Legend holds that Izta was an Aztec princess who died of a broken heart upon hearing falsely that her sweetheart, Popocatepetl, had died in battle. When Popo returned from war, finding his Izta dead, he built a high pyramid for her and one for himself. Mexicans say that Popo stands guard over princess Izta. Have students rewrite the legend of Popo and Izta giving another explanation for the origin of the two volcanoes.

Spanish Search Center

Let your *estudiantes* develop their own Spanish vocabulary center. After making a list of common Spanish words (color words and number words, for example) and their meanings, have students use graph paper to hide their words in a word search puzzle. Below each puzzle, have students list the **meanings** of the words to look for. Laminate puzzles and place at a center with plastic marks or overhead projector pens. For self-checking, have each puzzle-maker provide an answer key of the hidden words.

verde—green	sol—sun	uno—one
rojo—red	día—day	dos—two
negro—black	noche—night	tres—three
azul—blue	gracias—thank-you	cuatro—four
blanco—white	hola—hello	cinco—five
moreno—brown	adiós—good-bye	seis—six
	gato—cat	siete—seven
	perro—dog	ocho—eight
		nueve –nine
		diez—ten

Let's Get Packin'

All you need to culminate a study of Mexico's land and climate are an old suitcase and plenty of resource books. Divide the class into five groups and assign each a region of Mexico: Northern Mexico, Central Plateau, Yucatán Peninsula, East Coast, Southern Mexico. After research, students compile a packing list of clothing, recreational equipment, and supplies to take on a trip to that region. Students bring items on their list from home or draw pictures. In turn, each group packs the suitcase and goes through its contents with the rest of the class, giving reasons for their selections.

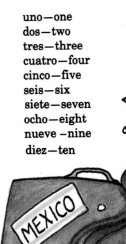

MEXICO

135

Vocabulario Español

Circle the Spanish words in the word search.
Check them off in the Word Bank as used.

```
R C E S C U C H A L U C I L E P B I B L I O B A
O O J T O E X A P C O E C A R A C H N C T A I L
M R E N Y A C E A M I S M P O L P A I E E S B M
A R S C A I M N G D A P A B R L U E C O S N L E
N E S I S M A T I M E A T U E P E L A M C I I E
U C U U S E V I N L I N U R C E R G O C U R O R
M T M V D E C H A S S O S L E C T U R A C O T E
M A I E E X L A E L A L E I S A A F U E H V E T
U M D N L A P I Z S P T V C O L D H C S E A C N
L E I T E M L L I A S A C H M U L H A A N F A A
A N O A E E R G N L R A L M U E R Z O I Z R M I
H T M N A N D I N G I S I L B E R R O C A O U D
C E A A L A N G U A G B E N C O T A C N I P C U
A L S G O T R E V E S C R I T U R A L E R Y H T
H I P S E L G N I P A Z I O A N N A E I A N A S
C B E I N G C O R R E M V S L V E N T C N M C E
U R L L S E L A I C O S S O I D U T S E A B H S
M P I Z A R R A P E L I A C I T A M E T A M R A
T P L I C A C I O B B D H O O H C A H C U M N L
N U M E R O O L P R O F E S O R A L E U C S E C
```

Word Bank

examen	(test)	por favor	(please)
lápiz	(pencil)	escuchen	(listen)
libro	(book)	correctamente	(correctly)
receso	(recess)	matemática	(mathematics)
lectura	(reading)	almuerzo	(lunch)
escritura	(writing)	página	(page)
ciencia	(science)	casa	(house)
estudios sociales	(social studies)	ventana	(window)
música	(music)	puerta	(door)
idioma	(language)	pizarra	(blackboard)
inglés	(English)	película	(movie)
español	(Spanish)	biblioteca	(library)
escuela	(school)	número	(number)
profesora	(teacher)	muchacho	(boy)
clase	(class)	muchacha	(girl)
		estudiante	(student)

Matador Magic

Cut out the nine strips. Paste to a red construction paper cape in the correct order.

A bullfight is an exciting contest of daring and skill. It begins with the parade of the *matador* and his assistants into the bullring. They are led by an elegant horseman on a handsome steed. Then the bull comes rushing in. As the matador approaches him, he begins graceful moves with his cape. These moves bring cheers from the crowd.

Next the *picador* enters the ring on horseback. Three times he pokes a long pole into the bull's shoulders. Then a bugle is blown. This announces the *banderillero* who runs toward the bull and pushes *banderillas*, sharp sticks decorated with colored ribbons, into his neck.

The matador now makes repeated passes with a sword hidden behind his cape. He plunges the sword into the bull's neck, and the bull falls dead. The fight is finished, and the crowd cheers.

Best of *THE MAILBOX* ● *INTERMEDIATE* ● ©The Education Center, Inc. ● Rebecca Simpson, Winston-Salem, NC   Keys pp. 189-191

The banderillero pushes three sticks into the bull.	
The matador and his assistants enter the ring.	The picador pokes the bull with a pole.
The bull enters the ring.	The picador enters the ring.
The matador gracefully moves his cape.	A bugle is blown.
The matador kills the bull.	The matador moves with a hidden sword.

Pattern

Enlarge and use with "Mexican Hall Of Fame" on page 135.

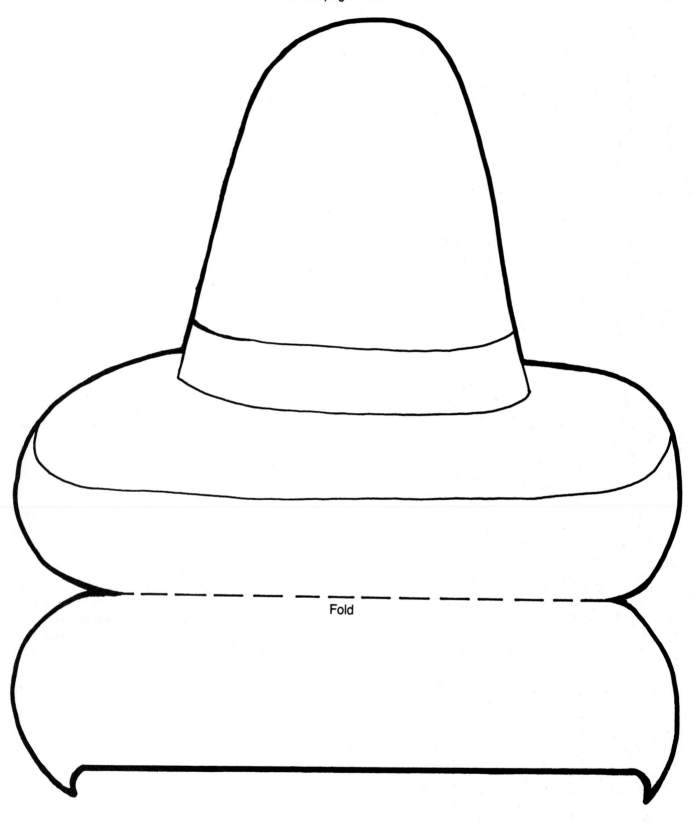

Fold

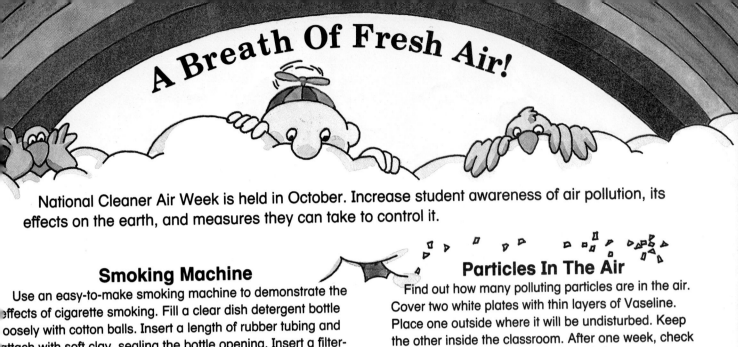

A Breath Of Fresh Air!

National Cleaner Air Week is held in October. Increase student awareness of air pollution, its effects on the earth, and measures they can take to control it.

Smoking Machine

Use an easy-to-make smoking machine to demonstrate the effects of cigarette smoking. Fill a clear dish detergent bottle loosely with cotton balls. Insert a length of rubber tubing and attach with soft clay, sealing the bottle opening. Insert a filter-less cigarette and light it. After squeezing the bottle several times, students can see the discoloration that occurs.

Deborah DeLuccia
North Haledon, NJ

Effects Of Pollution On Clothing

Cut discarded nylon hose into small equal squares. Fasten each square between two sticks to spread the hose apart. Place the samples in several different locations. (Remember to keep one inside as a control.) Check each one daily to see how quickly holes form. What does this tell you about clothes people wear in heavily polluted areas?

Destruction By Pollution

The gases in polluted air will slowly destroy a natural rubber band. Wrap several rubber bands around a coat hanger. Hang outdoors in a shady area. Keep a few rubber bands in a box in the room as a control. After nine days, examine the rubber bands from outside with a magnifying glass. Look for cracks and dried places. How do they compare with the control?

Particles In The Air

Find out how many polluting particles are in the air. Cover two white plates with thin layers of Vaseline. Place one outside where it will be undisturbed. Keep the other inside the classroom. After one week, check each plate. You might use a magnifying glass to examine particles. How do the plates compare with each other? Are there any particles in the room? Which plate shows greater evidence of air pollution? Where did the particles come from? What could be done about pollution-producing factories?

What Happens To Plants

Tie clear plastic bags around two young plants. Spray deodorant from an aerosol can into one. What effect does it have? What do you think pollution does to the plants we eat?

How Much Do Cars Really Pollute?

Attach a piece of white construction paper or cardboard to a long stick, and cover the paper with Vaseline. Carefully hold the stick so the cardboard is about one foot from the exhaust pipe of a car. Have someone start the car, making sure you stand away from the exhaust. After a few minutes, check for an accumulation of carbon particles on the paper. Are the results surprising? Now think about the cars in your city. What could be done to reduce air pollution caused by cars?

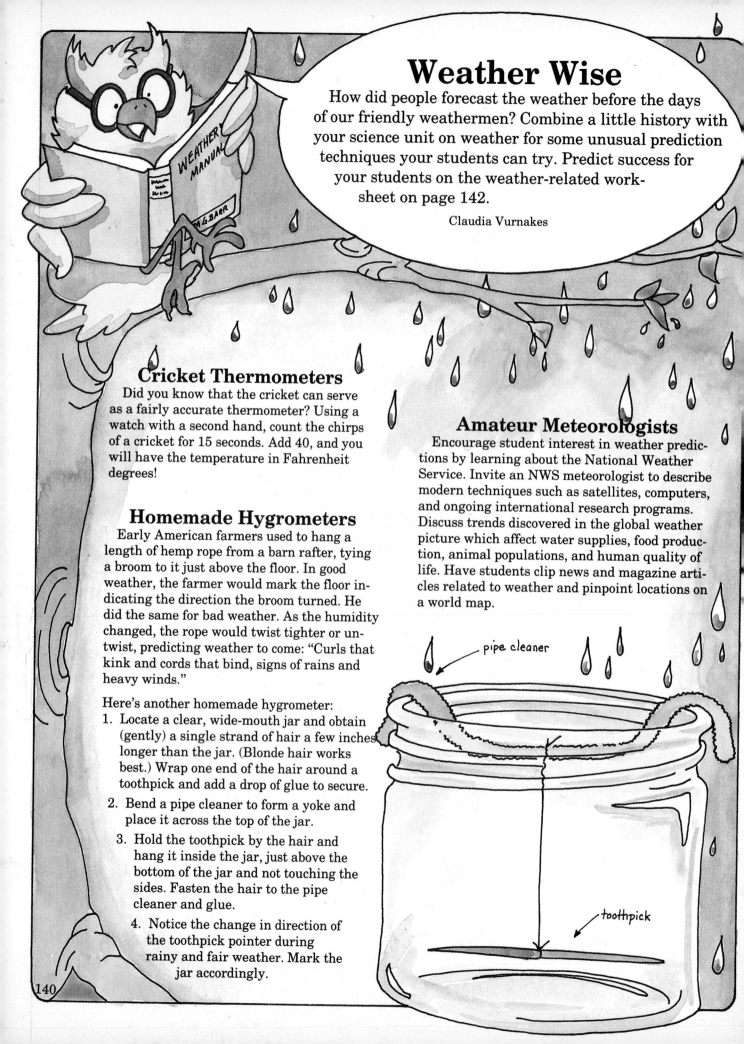

Weather Wise

How did people forecast the weather before the days of our friendly weathermen? Combine a little history with your science unit on weather for some unusual prediction techniques your students can try. Predict success for your students on the weather-related worksheet on page 142.

Claudia Vurnakes

Cricket Thermometers

Did you know that the cricket can serve as a fairly accurate thermometer? Using a watch with a second hand, count the chirps of a cricket for 15 seconds. Add 40, and you will have the temperature in Fahrenheit degrees!

Homemade Hygrometers

Early American farmers used to hang a length of hemp rope from a barn rafter, tying a broom to it just above the floor. In good weather, the farmer would mark the floor indicating the direction the broom turned. He did the same for bad weather. As the humidity changed, the rope would twist tighter or untwist, predicting weather to come: "Curls that kink and cords that bind, signs of rains and heavy winds."

Here's another homemade hygrometer:
1. Locate a clear, wide-mouth jar and obtain (gently) a single strand of hair a few inches longer than the jar. (Blonde hair works best.) Wrap one end of the hair around a toothpick and add a drop of glue to secure.

2. Bend a pipe cleaner to form a yoke and place it across the top of the jar.

3. Hold the toothpick by the hair and hang it inside the jar, just above the bottom of the jar and not touching the sides. Fasten the hair to the pipe cleaner and glue.

4. Notice the change in direction of the toothpick pointer during rainy and fair weather. Mark the jar accordingly.

Amateur Meteorologists

Encourage student interest in weather predictions by learning about the National Weather Service. Invite an NWS meteorologist to describe modern techniques such as satellites, computers, and ongoing international research programs. Discuss trends discovered in the global weather picture which affect water supplies, food production, animal populations, and human quality of life. Have students clip news and magazine articles related to weather and pinpoint locations on a world map.

pipe cleaner

toothpick

aluminum foil

lid

plastic tub

Winning Weather Vanes

Every pioneer learned to look first at the direction of the wind to predict the weather. Your students may enjoy making silhouettes of common early American weather vanes, after hearing about the most famous vane of all. Legend has it that Ben Franklin, when abroad, was asked to prove that he was from Boston. A single mention of the grasshopper weather vane atop Boston's Faneuil Hall was all it took.

Here's a weather vane your students can make:
1. Straighten the hook of a wire coat hanger.
2. Cover ½ of the hanger with aluminum foil. Cut foil 1″ wider than wire outline, fold over edges, and tape.
3. Fill a pint-size plastic tub with packed sand and snap on the lid.
4. Poke the coat hanger through the lid, and push it down in the sand so the stem touches the container bottom. The weather vane should turn freely.
5. Mark north, south, east, and west on the container with a marker. Place the weather vane in an open area to catch the wind. Use a compass to line up the weather vane properly. The open half of the vane will always point in the direction from which the wind is coming.

Weather Sayings

Perhaps the oldest weather knowledge has been handed down in the form of rhymes and sayings. These bits of folklore developed as early Americans observed conditions around them. Their very lives depended on interpreting weather signs correctly. Here's a list of sayings that are fairly accurate in predicting the weather.

— When the bees stay near the hive, rain is close by.
— Flies will swarm before a storm.
— Halos around the moon or sun mean that rain will surely come.
— When forest murmurs and mountain roars, close your windows and shut your doors.
— Moss dry, sunny sky; moss wet, rain you'll get.
— When smoke descends, good weather ends.
— A cow's tail to the west is weather coming at its best; a cow's tail to the east is weather coming at its least.
— Crows gathered around the ground, a sign that rain will soon come down.
— Red sky at night, sailor's delight; red sky at morning, sailors take warning.

• Have each student draw a weather poster depicting a saying. Can other students "read" the weather indicated?
• Bring several almanacs to class and ask students to list interesting forecasts. Have students interview older family members for local weather wisdom and compile your own class almanac.

Weather Watch

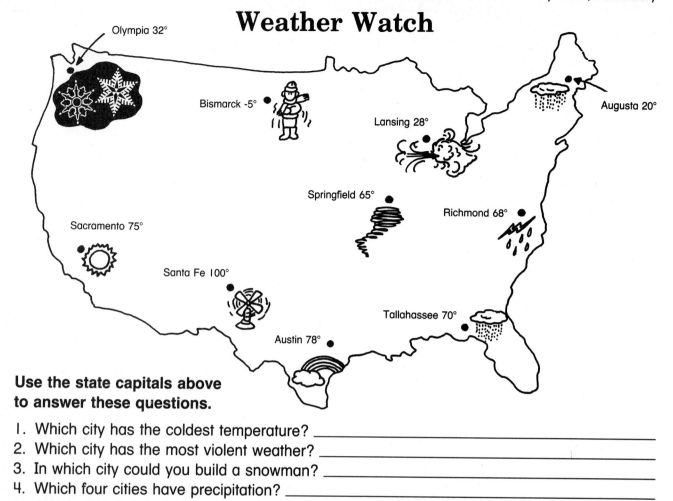

Use the state capitals above to answer these questions.

1. Which city has the coldest temperature? _____
2. Which city has the most violent weather? _____
3. In which city could you build a snowman? _____
4. Which four cities have precipitation? _____
5. Which city has the highest temperature? _____
6. Where is there a thunderstorm? _____
7. Which cities have strong winds? _____
8. Which city shows the temperature at which water freezes? _____
9. Which city has the most colorful weather word? _____

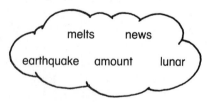

melts   news
earthquake   amount   lunar

What is most useful when it's used up?

lightning   up   ray
blizzard   atmosphere

1. Dangerous, blowing snowstorm _____
2. Word referring to the moon _____
3. A shaking of the earth _____
4. Used to describe how much rainfall _____
5. Air surrounding the earth _____

6. Flash of light in a thunderstorm _____
7. Where you look to see clouds _____
8. Thin beam of light from sun _____
9. What snow does when temperature rises
   _____
10. TV show on which weather report is heard
   _____

Now write the first letter of each answer in the blank with the same number.

___ ___ ___ ___ ___ ___ ___ ___ ___ ___
 5   10   7   9   1   8   3   2   6   4

The Dancing Snake

Pretend to be a snake handler or magician as you use the principle of static electricity to make a dancing snake.

Dr. Hy Kim
Pittsburg State University
Pittsburg, KS

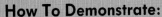

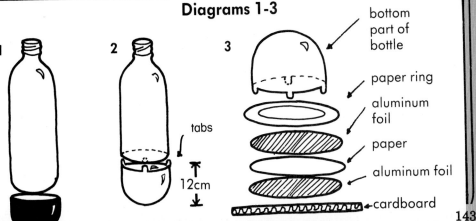

What You'll Need:
two-liter pop bottle
ruler marked in cm
scissors
aluminum foil
tape
two sheets of paper
glue
tissue paper
felt pen
cardboard
wool cloth

How To Make:

1. As shown in diagram 1, remove the black bottom from the pop bottle. This may be done by filling the bottle with hot water (not hot enough to melt the plastic) and setting the bottle in hot water. Wait a minute or two. The hot water should soften the glue so the black part may be easily pulled away from the bottle.

2. Mark the bottle 13 centimeters (cm) from the bottom. Cut around the bottle evenly at the mark. Trim off a one-centimeter strip, leaving four tabs. (See diagram 2.)

3. Cut out two circles of aluminum foil and two circles of paper each with a diameter that is two centimeters wider than the diameter of the bottle. Cut out the center of one of the paper circles to make a paper ring.

4. Glue the materials together in the order shown in diagram 3, beginning at the bottom.

5. Make a paper snake by cutting tissue paper in a spiral. (See illustration.) Use a felt pen to mark its eyes and mouth.

6. Place the snake inside the paper ring. Set the inverted bottle over the snake and tape the four tabs to the paper ring. Construction of the snake cage is now complete.

How To Demonstrate:

You are ready for your performance. Rub the cage dome with a wool cloth or piece of fur for a couple of minutes. The snake will move up and down inside the cage. Sometimes you'll need to shake the cage so that the snake will fall to the bottom. Try making snakes of varying lengths in order to find the size that keeps the snake dancing rather than attached to the dome. Plan your performance for a clear, dry day because it won't work very well on rainy or humid days.

Why This Works:

Static electricity is produced when an object gains or loses negative charges. When you rub the plastic bottle with wool or fur, the plastic becomes negatively charged, and the wool becomes positively charged. Extra electrons accumulate in the plastic dome and attract the snake, which is neutral at first. Once the snake touches the dome, it is negatively charged too. Like charges repel each other, so the snake falls to the bottom of the cage. The aluminum foil in the bottom of the cage is a good conductor for discharging the extra electrons from the snake. Then the snake is attracted to the negatively charged dome and the cycle begins again.

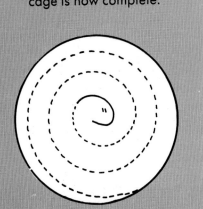

Diagrams 1-3

1

2

tabs

12cm

3

bottom part of bottle

paper ring

aluminum foil

paper

aluminum foil

cardboard

PLANTS, PLANTS EVERYWHERE!

Wherever life exists—from the frozen Arctic to the steamy tropics, from high atop a mountain to the ocean deep—plants are there. Let the following activities lead your students outdoors for a closer look at the world of plants.

Ideas by Amy Bense

PROVE IT WITH PLANTS

Without plants, there would be no life on the earth. They provide the oxygen we breathe and are an important source of food, clothing, and shelter. Photosynthesis is the process by which plants combine light energy, water, minerals from the soil, and carbon dioxide from the air to produce food and release oxygen. Demonstrate various stages of this process with the following easy-to-do experiments:

Experiment #1

To illustrate the need for carbon dioxide in photosynthesis, spread a thin layer of petroleum jelly on both sides of several plant leaves. Place the plant in sunlight for two or three days. Have students compare the leaves covered with petroleum jelly to the leaves that were left uncovered.

Experiment #2

In photosynthesis, chlorophyll in the leaves absorbs light energy from the sun. Give students a close-up look at chloroplasts, the plant cells that contain chlorophyll. Mount a tiny piece of an elodea leaf (an aquarium plant available at most pet stores) on a slide. Focus under low power and have students note their observations. Can students locate any chloroplasts? What shape are the cells?

To further illustrate the presence of chlorophyll in green plants, boil several spinach leaves or broccoli spears in a pot of water. Have students observe the color of the water after boiling for several minutes.

Experiment #3

Chlorophyll needs energy from the sun in order to manufacture food. Show the plant's need for sunlight by clipping two, small squares of black construction paper to the opposite sides of a growing leaf. Place the plant in sunlight. Be sure to keep the soil moist. Remove the paper in three or four days. Have students observe the color of the leaf. How does it compare to the leaves that were left uncovered?

Experiment #4

The food formed by photosynthesis is used for growth and repair, or it is stored in special areas in the stems or roots. Many plants store food as starch. To test for starch in plants, divide your students into small groups. Give each group the following materials: small pieces of a potato and a carrot; a lettuce and a cabbage leaf; a stalk of celery, a green bean and a kidney bean; an eyedropper; dilute iodine solution; paper towels; rubber gloves. Have students place each vegetable on a paper towel. Instruct one student in each group to place two or three drops of iodine on each plant part. (Provide rubber gloves for safety.) If starch is present, the iodine will turn blue-black in color. Have students record the results on a chart.

WILDFLOWER COLLECTIONS

Students tire of the traditional leaf collections. How about a class wildflower collection instead? As students bring in wildflowers they've collected, lay the flowers flat between newspapers. Place several books on top to press flowers for three to four days. Use identification books to find each flower's common name and scientific classification. Flowers look great mounted in a photo album or on cardboard covered with laminating film. Be sure to remind students not to pick from parks or nature trails since these flowers might be endangered.

American Pasqueflower
Anemone Patens

PLANT PEOPLE

Inject some creative-writing fun into your plants unit. Remove the top one-fourth of an eggshell. Rinse out the remaining shell. Use markers to draw a funny face on the shell. Fill the eggshell with soil and a few herb seeds. Keep the soil watered and watch your plant person grow hair!

Have each student name his plant person and write a story about "The Invasion of the Plant People." Bind the completed stories in a class book. Display the plant people in egg cartons.

FLIP BOOKS

A study of plants opens the door to a wide variety of research topics. Instead of the standard one-page reports, let your students try writing flip books. To make a flip book, cut several pieces of art paper to a desired size, punch holes in the top of each sheet, and tie the pages together with yarn. Students can now turn their reports into original picture books, adding their own illustrations to each page of information. Try the following topics or have students investigate an area of their choice.

Sample topics

The Importance of Plants	Plants of the Tropical Rain Forest
Flowering Plants	Desert Plants
Cone-bearing Plants	Saltwater Plants
Ferns	Freshwater Plants
Photosynthesis	Pollination
How Seeds Are Made	Parts of a Flower
How Seeds Are Scattered	How Flowering Plants Reproduce
Liverworts and Mosses	Vegetative Propagation
Algae	Insect-eating Plants
Fungi	Plant Diseases and Pests
Plants of the Forests	Greenhouses
	How to Make a Terrarium

PRODUCE A PLANT

For a fun review game, divide your class into three teams. Tape a piece of white construction paper on the board for each team. In turn, ask a team member a review question. If the student answers correctly, she draws part of a flower on her team's paper. Each team must draw, in order, the following parts: a stem, two sepals, petals, a pistil and ovary, a stigma, and two stamens. The first team to complete their flower is the winner.

Team A   Team B   Team C

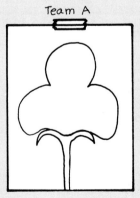  

(The Winners!)

Solar Fun

With summer coming up and children spending more time outdoors, a set of solar energy experiments could be just the thing! These activities will demonstrate the power and potential uses of our sun, as well as methods of gathering and storing its energy. Experiments may be used as class projects, by small groups, or as individual assignments.

Solar Cooking
Use the sun to cook a hot dog!

Materials:
1 hot dog
poster board
a cardboard box plus extra cardboard
aluminum foil
flat black paint
an unpainted coat hanger
rubber cement
2 small nuts and bolts
tape

1. Cut the box as shown.

poke holes for nuts and bolts

2. Cut two cardboard pieces in this shape to fit inside the box.

holes for nuts and bolts

3. Glue a smooth piece of aluminum foil to one side of the poster board. Tape it to the two cardboard pieces as shown.

tape

poster board covered with aluminum foil

tape

4. Insert a coat hanger through the hot dog, then through the cardboard holes.

5. Use the nuts and bolts to attach cardboard pieces to the box.

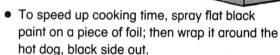

coat hanger through holes in cardboard and box and through hot dog

- To speed up cooking time, spray flat black paint on a piece of foil; then wrap it around the hot dog, black side out.

- Keep hot dog aimed at the sun to reflect as much solar energy as possible.

- Turn hot dog to cook evenly.

- On a warm sunny day the hot dog should take about 15 minutes to cook.

How many hot dogs could you cook in three hours? What other kinds of food could you cook in the sun? Would this be an expensive or inexpensive means of cooking?

Sun-dried Raisins
Dry fruit with solar energy!

Materials:
¼ lb. seedless grapes
cardboard
a plastic window screen cut in half
a food scale
string
masking tape
pencil and paper

1. Cut a hole in the cardboard and tape one screen half in place as shown.

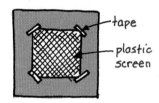

tape

plastic screen

2. Weigh the grapes. Record the weight.

3. Place grapes on the screen. Tape the second half of screen on top.

grapes

plastic screen

cardboard

4. Hang in a sunny place outside or in a window.

5. After about two weeks, remove the grapes and weigh them.

- What do you have now?
- Why do the grapes weigh less after drying?
- How does drying food preserve it?
- Would drying be an expensive method for food preservation?

Hot And Cool Colors

Discover which colors store more heat.

Materials:

ice cubes
a measuring cup
sandwich-size plastic bags
a watch
sheets of white, black, green, red, blue
  construction paper
chart and pencil

1. Put one ice cube in each bag.
2. Place one bag on top of each color of paper.
3. Place bags and papers in a sunny location.
4. After 20 minutes, measure the water in each bag.

Which one had the most water?
Which would be cooler—a house with a white roof or a house with a dark roof?

Color of Paper	Amount of Water
Black	
White	
Red	
Green	
Blue	

Storing Solar Energy

Compare the abilities of different materials to store heat.

Materials:

4 small metal cans (same size)
4 thermometers
black paint
paintbrush
a cardboard box
sand, water, salt, shredded paper
chart and pencil

1. Fill each can with a different material.

2. Paint the box black, let it dry, put the cans in it, and close the top. Place it in the sun.

3. After 30 minutes, remove the cans. Place a thermometer in each.

4. Measure and record the temperature on each thermometer after two, four, six, eight, and ten minutes.

Which temperature fell most slowly?
Which material stores solar energy best?
What materials would be good to construct solar collectors from?

	2 min.	4 min.	6 min.	8 min.	10 min.
Sand					
Salt					
Water					
Paper					

OUR READERS WRITE

Welcome Puzzle

Help your students learn their classmates' names with this word search puzzle. Draw a large numeral to represent their grade and inside it list all students' names, hidden among other letters. Keep the students working while you're busy with first-day paperwork.

Grace Conway
Hillside, NJ

Friday Letters

Each Friday, the children in my class write letters to me. They use correct letter form and may write whatever they wish—what they liked or didn't like during the week, problems with friends, questions about schoolwork, etc. Letters go in a "Friday Letters" mailbox. Over the weekend, I answer each letter so children receive a reply on Monday. This gives children who have a hard time opening up an opportunity to express themselves.

D. Shelton
Memphis, TN

Class Movie

At the beginning of the school year I use the school's videotape recorder/player to start our own class movie. During the year I tape different activities (book reports, parties, plays, songs). At the end of the school year we have hours of "memories" to enjoy.

Helene Sparaco
Middleburg, NY

Bulletin Board Storage

A clear dress bag is a super place to store bulletin boards. You can see what's inside and get to it easily.

Yvonne Hornbuckle
Huntsville, AL

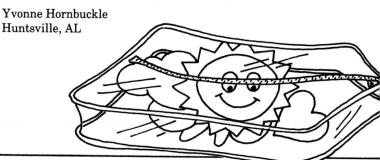

Creative Writing Notebook

Instruct each student to use a spiral notebook for creative writings. The student writes the first copy of a story/writing on the back side of a page and the final, corrected copy on the front side of the next page in the notebook. This eliminates turning back and forth when editing the final copy. My students like this method of rewriting stories.

Bonnie jo Kyles
Ennis, MT

Pizza Prize

Motivate good classroom behavior with this delicious idea. Cut out a large, white poster board circle. Divide it into 16 sections to look like a pizza. Each time your class exhibits outstanding behavior, color one slice red. When every slice is colored, reward your class with a pizza party! English muffins covered with bottled pizza sauce and shredded cheese make tasty, inexpensive pizzas.

Mary Larson
Bristol, CT

Preserve Your Posters

Are you sick of peeling the tape off the backs of your posters until you soon have no poster left? Here is a cheap and simple solution for preserving your posters. On the back of each poster, stick down large pieces of masking tape. Then, whenever you put up your poster, all you need to do is place curls of tape right on top of the tape strips on the back of each poster. This keeps your posters looking as good as new!

Kathy M. Peterson
Alpha, IL

Masking Tape

Person on your left reads

Gray Lundy

Skip two cards

Teacher's Turn

What's The Order?

Use a card system for a change of pace in choosing student reading order. Label cards with students' names. Also include cards with directions such as: person on your left reads, skip two cards, read again, choose a boy, teacher's turn, free choice, etc. After each child reads, he picks up a card to determine the next reader.

Jeane Cowin
Elmore, MN

Display Space

Running out of display space? Tie one end of a piece of yarn to a jumbo paper clip and the other end to a metal clothespin. Slip the paper clip end between the metal strips and the panels in your ceiling so that the clothespin end hangs down. Clip work up using the clothespin.

Sandra Gray
Gaithersburg, MD

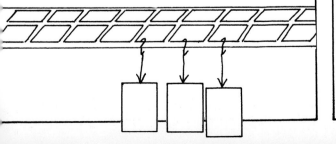

Tackle Box Tote

An old fishing tackle box makes a handy container for school supplies! Use small compartments for stickers or paper clips. The slender sections will hold pencils, markers, or scissors. Store tape and glue in the lower compartment. Carried between home and school, it will help avoid duplicate purchases of expensive supplies.

Paula Holdren
Prospect, KY

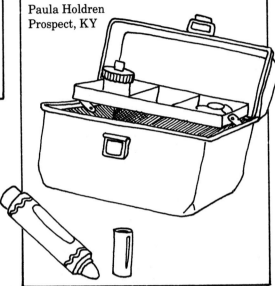

Laminated "Yard Goods"

Preprinted, colorful yard goods material makes a creative display item. Find material printed with Snoopy, Annie, Smurfs, Care Bears, or anything related to a center or unit theme. Laminate it to make very attractive bulletin board or learning center figures. After it is laminated, the wrong side of the fabric is still pretty enough to mount the figure in a window for a two-sided effect.

Marcille Covey
Lawton, OK

Language Challenge

Make a game out of learning the parts of speech. Have students think of a noun, verb, and adjective that begin with the first letter of each class member's name.

O.J. Robertson
Russell Springs, KY

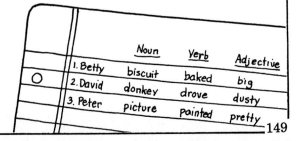

	Noun	Verb	Adjective
1. Betty	biscuit	baked	big
2. David	donkey	drove	dusty
3. Peter	picture	painted	pretty

Homework Excuse Note

If you have students who do not turn in work, have them write an excuse note. Let students know it will be on file to look at when a question about low grades comes up.

Lynn Franklin
Savannah, GA

I did not have my homework because I had to to the doctor. I had a cold. Sue

I did not have my homework because I left my books on the bus. Corey

Marker "Pawns"

I never throw away the caps of worn-out markers. Instead, I keep them and put them in the envelope of any new game I construct, to be used as game pawns or markers. They come in all colors, so it is easy for a child to recognize his own pawn in the game. Best of all, they cost nothing, and I always have some handy if one gets lost.

Helen Burkard
Beckley, WV

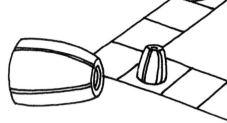

Calculator Week

The week before Christmas vacation makes a great "Calculator Week." Children bring calculators from home. Each day we learn about a calculator function and play a calculator game or complete a worksheet designed for a calculator. The children think they are "getting out of work," and I have no math papers to grade.

Cindy Newell
Durant, OK

Tall Tale Box

When studying tall tales, legends, and exaggeration, provide your students with a Tall Tale Box. Students fill the box with their own exaggerated stories or statements, such as "If I exercise any harder, my feet will fall off." At the end of your study, award an oversized sucker or candy bar to the writer of the "tallest" tall tale.

Rhonda Thurman-Rice
Catoosa, OK

Scrambled Shapes

Two of our readers came up with variations on the same idea. Kathy Kuehn of Amery, WI, runs duplicates of seasonal shapes and scrambles one of the week's spelling words on each. At Halloween, the shapes are ghosts, witches, cats, and at Christmas she uses trees, Santas, deer, etc.

Marilyn Janssen of Lorraine, KS, also cuts out holiday shapes, but programs them with scrambled seasonal words. For example, she labels a Christmas tree shape with the letters OSTY for her students to rearrange into the word TOYS.

Kathy Kuehn
Amery, WI

Marilyn Janssen
Lorraine, KS

Test Treat

Try giving students a treat during a test. I provide popcorn for each child. It soothes nervousness and makes the situation more relaxed. Pop the corn and fill a bag for inexpensive, nutritional fun!

Sr. Ann Claire Rhoads
Emmitsburg, MD

Masking Tape Hanger

You can use masking tape to hang papers on a cinder block wall. Attach a long strip of tape along the wall; then push straight pins down through the student's paper and the tape. The tape strip can be used over and over for several months.

Sandy Latham
Atlanta, GA

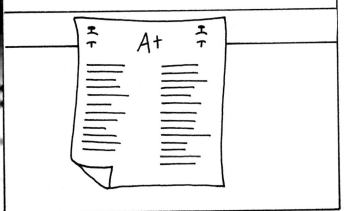

Manners Count

Influence your students' use of good manners with this positive-reinforcement approach. Assign one student to make a mark on a card each time he hears another student say, "Please," "Thank-you," "Excuse me," or any of a number of comments you have decided to reward. Then reward your class with one extra minute of recess time for each ten polite comments recorded. This certainly sharpens their awareness of good manners.

Kathy Beard
Keystone Heights, FL

Leftover Lifesaver

Put restless students and leftover supplies to work for you! Mount white background paper on a bulletin board. Place half-used markers, pens, stickers, and other leftover materials in a box. When students finish their work, let them use the supplies to decorate the board. You'll finish the year with a creative bulletin board and fewer "leftovers" to pack away.

Class Flag

Promote a feeling of class unity by designing a "class flag." This may be a community design or a series of squares of individual designs based on a theme such as "Our Favorite Things."

Susan Chisari
Orlando, FL

Tax Tip For Teachers

Keep a yellow highlighter pen handy so you can mark in your checkbook any purchases for school materials, books, or your *Mailbox* and *Worksheet Magazine* subscriptions. The highlighted checks are easy to find when calculating business expenses at tax time.

Clarese A. Rehn
Lake Villa, IL

Lamination Shortcut

Avoid problems in cutting out small items that have been laminated on one side only. Place the item on the film as usual. Now place a piece of scrap paper (such as newspaper) directly over the item. With scissors, cut around the item as closely as possible. The scrap paper backing will peel right off!

Karen Stockstill
Sidney, OH

Congratulations Poster

Recognize student achievements on a congratulations poster displayed outside your classroom door. Laminate the poster and list student accomplishments with an overhead-marking pen. Use a damp cloth to keep the list up-to-date. Students will glow with pride!

Debbie Wiggins
Myrtle Beach, SC

Easy Change

Open-ended gameboards or centers that need to use pictures can be easily changed if both board and pictures are laminated and glued together with rubber cement. The cement holds well until the picture needs to be changed, then peels right off.

Mary Vander Poppen
Seattle, WA

All Keyed Up

I use old discarded keys (from cars, doors, locks) as pawns for trail games. They are a hit, especially with the boys, who enjoy "driving" around a game. Old games that had become dust-collectors are now popular choices.

Nancy Johnson
Greensboro, NC

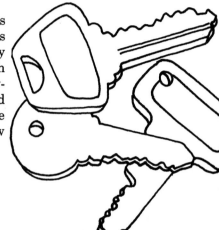

Field Trip Puzzle

Use this idea to keep students busy during a long bus ride. Develop a puzzle similar to the one shown, adapting items for the area through which you will travel. Give each child a copy and a stub of a crayon. As each student spots a listed item, he colors that section of the puzzle.

Carole Pippert
Laurel, MD

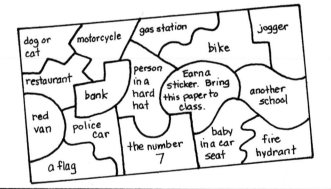

Where's The Pencil?

Are the pencils always disappearing from the office sign-in sheet or the library checkout area? Buy three-inch bridge pencils and keep them in a small basket. They are inexpensive and rarely will anyone wander off with one by mistake.

Sandy Docca
Silver Spring, MD

Easy-to-Make Holiday Centers

Look for two-sided decorations in discount department stores during holiday seasons. Use sticky dots to make a game trail on the front of the decoration. Glue on a holiday gift tag with the name of the game and directions. Laminate the decoration. Put a clear pocket on the back to hold question cards. Your holiday center is ready for use.

Mary Anne Haffner
Waynesboro, PA

152

Clinkers

An interesting approach to literature is the discussion of exactly what makes a "bad" book. Children share their ideas, and usually a lively discussion ensues. I then encourage the kids to bring in "clinkers" to share. The books are placed in a basket in the reading corner. Sooner or later we discover that "one man's trash is another man's treasure."

Paula K. Holdren
Prospect, KY

Poems To The President

To motivate my class on their handwriting and to further their interest in patriotism, I sent the best copies of a poem that we had copied to the president. In return, we received a nice letter, a book on the White House, and a picture of President Reagan. The children loved it and learned a great deal in the process.

Mary Ellen Bailey
Springfield, MO

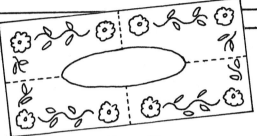

Tissue Box Corners

This suggestion is for further use from a tissue box. Many brands use a flower motif on the top. Corners can be cut from the top of the box to be used directly on bulletin boards as decorative corners.

Ann F. Fausnight
Canton, OH

Pretty Bulletin Boards

To encourage children who continually fail to finish their work and to reward the children who always finish, I use a monthly art project.

At the beginning of each month, on a large piece of poster board, I draw the outlined shape of something seasonal such as an Easter egg.

As each child finishes his work paper and brings it to me, I give him a piece of colored tissue paper (about one-inch square). He takes the tissue paper to the art project, folds it around the bottom of a large primary crayon (see illustration), and pastes the tissue on the Easter egg.

No one wants to miss pasting on their piece and as the outline becomes nearly filled in, students become eager to get it finished. This really helps motivate everyone to finish their work, and I get a pretty, new bulletin board every month!

Lynn Klomfar
St. Petersburg, FL

End-of-the Year Auction

During the school year students accumulate points to spend in an auction. On a card for each child, keep track of points given for class chores, extra-credit assignments, etc. At the end of the year, clean out cupboards, shelves, and closets. Allow children to bid on the discarded books, plants, posters, markers, games, or other donated items. Deduct points on student cards as the auction continues. Provide a mystery item for final bids.

Karen Nider
Dansville, NY

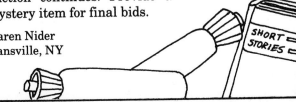

153

Number Potions

Brew up some number magic with these recipes from Elizabeth Cole of Annapolis, MD. Write on index cards for your math center, or give to the class orally for a Halloween treat!

Number Potion #1

1. Choose any number.
2. Multiply by 9. $276 \times 9 = 2484$
3. Add the numbers in the product. $2 + 4 + 8 + 4 = 18$
4. The sum of the numbers can always be divided by 9 without a remainder. $18 \div 9 = 2$

Number Potion #2

1. Choose any number.   12
2. Multiply by 5. $12 \times 5 = 60$
3. Add 6 to the product. $60 + 6 = 66$
4. Multiply the sum by 4. $66 \times 4 = 264$
5. Add 9 to the product. $264 + 9 = 273$
6. Multiply the sum by 5. $273 \times 5 = 1365$
7. Cross off the last 2 digits.   1365̶
8. Subtract 1 from the result. $13 - 1 = 12$

The answer should be the number you started with.

Number Potion #3

1. Choose any number.   11
2. Multiply by 6. $11 \times 6 = 66$
3. Add 12 to the product. $66 + 12 = 78$
4. Divide the sum by 3. $78 \div 3 = 26$
5. Subtract 2 from the quotient. $26 - 2 = 24$
6. Divide the difference by 2. $24 \div 2 = 12$
7. Subtract the original number. $12 - 11 = 1$
8. Add 9 to the difference. $1 + 9 = 10$

The answer is always 10.

Number Potion #4

Challenge a friend to add eight 8s in such a way that the total is 1,000. If your friend gets stumped, show him to add the 8s like this:

$$8 + 8 + 8 + 88 + 888 = 1,000$$

Number Potion #5

1. Start with any number.   42
2. Change the order of the digits in any way you choose.   24
3. Subtract the smaller number from the larger number. $42 - 24 = 18$
4. The difference is always evenly divisible by 9! $18 \div 9 = 2$

Out-Of-The-Ordinary Math

After a long Christmas vacation, your students may need some "perking up." Why not welcome them back to school with an out-of-the-ordinary math lesson? Their enthusiasm for school will soar while they learn important math concepts.

Swiglies

Here's a math activity that teaches much more than numbers. Collect Styrofoam packing chips ("swiglies") or use dried beans. (You'll need several thousand, so start early!) Divide your class into groups of four to five students. Give each group a pencil, a writing tablet, and a large pile of swiglies. Tell the groups that they have only 20 minutes to count all their swiglies and that all group members must participate. Give no further instructions.

After ten minutes, stop the groups and discuss the different techniques used in counting. Point out the ways group members have tried to work together. If a group has not discovered a method that will work for them, discuss the techniques that have worked for other groups. Emphasize the importance of working together.

Not only will students practice counting by tens, hundreds, and thousands; they will also learn to work together, keep accurate records, and develop problem-solving strategies. And they'll have a great time doing it!

Sherry Ostroff
Lancaster, PA

Your Guess Is As Good As Mine

Even older students love guessing games. Sharpen estimating skills with these fun and challenging activities:

- How many words are on the front page of your local newspaper? Let students turn in their guesses; then begin the work of determining the winner. Cut the front page into small sections. Distribute one section to each of several small groups for counting. Every person must count and check the words in his group's section. After all groups have finished counting, write the total for each section on the board and add. The winner is the student with the closest estimate.

- Have students visit the library to estimate the number of books on the shelves. Then divide the class into small student teams. Each team will work together to develop a method for improving their estimates. Be sure to place a time limit for teams to turn in their guesses. Ask the librarian to supply the actual count to help determine the winning team.

- For a quick and easy change of pace, have students list some simple activities on the board: blink your eyes, write your name, count to ten, jump in place. Ask students to guess how many times they think they could complete the activity in one minute. When all guesses have been submitted, pair up students and have them conduct timed experiments to test their guesses. Post class "records" on a "One-Minute Records" bulletin board.

Math Posters

Turn kids on to the wonderful world of numbers with a monthly poster contest. Announce a new topic each month and provide plenty of poster board, paint, markers, and other supplies. Students can work on the posters during free time or at home. Display finished posters on a math bulletin board or in your school library. For an added incentive, ask a small group of faculty members to serve as judges. Award an inexpensive prize for the top poster of the month.

Possible Topics:
Math In My Life (how we use numbers)
Numbers In Sports (use of numbers in sports)
Math, Money And Me (economics)
Numbers In The News (current events)
Signs And Symbols In The World Of Math (math symbols)
The Language Of Math (math vocabulary)
The Shape Of Things (geometry)
Fractions Don't Frighten Me! (fractions)

Just Suppose . . .

. . . you want to get your math class in the holiday spirit! Write a puzzler on the board each day until Christmas for extra credit or a treat!

Sylvia Foust
Long Beach, NC

- . . . you need one yard of wrapping paper for every three gifts. If each student in the class wraps six gifts, how many yards of paper will be used? (Answer: 2 yd. per student × number of students)

- . . . a group of carolers walks five miles on each trip. How many miles will they walk if they go out each night for two school weeks? For the month of December? (Answers: 50 miles, 155 miles)

- . . . Santa receives 203 letters in one week. Each letter has a 25¢ stamp on it. How much is spent on stamps each day? How much would be spent if stamps were 15¢ each? (Answers: 29 letters/day, $7.25/day, $4.35 at 15¢)

- . . . you put three cranberries on one inch of string. Your tree needs nine feet of strung cranberries. How many cranberries will you need? How many berries for five trees? (Answers: 324 berries for 9 ft., 1620 for 5 trees)

- . . . a pine tree needs three gallons of water each day. How many quarts will it need for one week? How many gallons do seven trees need for one week? (Answers: 84 qt. per tree per wk., 147 gal. per wk. for 7 trees)

- . . . a candle burns in a house for two hours each night. How many hours will the candle have burned after 36 days? How many 24-hour periods is that? (Answers: 72 hr., three 24-hr. periods)

- . . . a reindeer has 20 teeth. If the number of teeth in a herd is 2940, how many reindeer are there? How many teeth would 50 reindeer have? (Answers: 147 reindeer, 1000 teeth)

- . . . ten feet of snow fall every day for four days. 16 feet melt. 12 feet fall the next day. The only way out is through your window, and it's four feet above the ground. How far up must you dig to get to the top of the snow? (Answer: 40−16 = 24+12 = 36−4 = 32 ft.)

- . . . there are 15 candy canes in a box for $1.37. You need one for everyone in school—495 kids! How much change will you get from a $50.00 bill? (Answers: 33 boxes, $4.79 in change)

- . . . you need three pounds of gingerbread dough to make one house. Half of the students in your class want to make four houses each. How many pounds of dough are needed? (Answer: 12 lb. per student × [number of students ÷ 2]) *+ (the number of students making [house] × 3 lbs)*

- . . . Santa has eaten 48 cookies in 12 years of his Christmas visits to your house. What was the average number of cookies that he ate on each visit? What will the total be three years from now? (Answers: 4 cookies/visit, 60 in 3 years)

- . . . 84 relatives are coming to your house for dinner! A 20-pound turkey will feed 14 people. Will you need more or fewer than ten turkeys? (Answer: fewer = 6 turkeys)

Number 9

When a number has been multiplied by 9, the sum of the digits in the answer is always 9.

$9 \times 2 = 18$ and $1 + 8 = 9$

$9 \times 6 = 54$ and $5 + 4 = 9$

$9 \times 271 = 2439$ and $2 + 4 + 3 + 9 = 18$ and $1 + 8 = 9$

To multiply any number by 9:
Add 0 to that number:
Subtract the original number:
And you'll have your answer:

$$9 \times \quad 34567$$
$$345670$$
$$- \ 34567$$
$$9 \times 34567 = 311103$$

If any number can be evenly divided by 9:

$$9 \overline{)\ 27639} \quad \frac{3071}{}$$

The digits of that number will add up to 9:

$$2 + 7 + 6 + 3 + 9 = 27$$
$$\text{and } 2 + 7 = 9$$

Why is the number 9 like a peacock?
Because it's nothing without a tail!

The number 9 can be made out of three whole matchsticks, without breaking or bending the matchsticks. Can you do it?

How would you write the number 100 with six nines?

$$99\, \frac{99}{99}$$

Ages & Ages

Some people don't like to tell how old they are.
Here's a way of finding out.
Ask a friend to *secretly* multiply his age by three.
Have him *secretly* add 6 to the answer.
Then he must divide the sum by 3
and tell you his answer.
(He will laugh since he knows the figure is not his true age.)
But, meanwhile, you *secretly* subtract 2 from his answer, and the result will always be your friend's true age.
(Now you laugh!)

An example:

$$\begin{array}{r} 9 \ \text{Age} \\ \times \ 3 \\ \hline 27 \\ + \ 6 \\ \hline 3\ \overline{)\ 33} \\ \hline 11 \\ - \ 2 \\ \hline 9 \end{array}$$

Write the year of your birth.
Double it.

Add 5.

Multiply by 50.

Add your age.

Add 365.

Subtract 615.

$$\begin{array}{r} 1956 \\ + \ 1956 \\ \hline 3912 \\ + \quad 5 \\ \hline 3917 \\ \times \quad 50 \\ \hline 195850 \\ + \quad 32 \\ \hline 195882 \\ + \quad 365 \\ \hline 196247 \\ - \quad 615 \\ \hline 195632 \end{array}$$

The first four digits will always be the year of your birth.

The last two digits will always be your age.

157

Calculator Crazies

Need a different kind of math center? Children punch out the answers to these riddles with a calculator. Write on tagboard and place in your math area.

What animal lays golden eggs?
- Start with 1000 of the animals.
- Multiply by 30 because they laid 30 eggs each.
- Subtract 20,000 because they stepped on that many eggs.
- Multiply by 3 because the farmer fed the animals 3 meals a day.
- Add 6006 because 6006 visitors took pictures of the animals.
- Subtract 1000 because the visitors bought 1000 eggs.
- Turn your calculator upside down to read the answer.

What part of your body do you stand on?
- Start with 6000 roller coaster seats.
- Subtract 1000 because that many people got on.
- Add 37 because only 37 people were brave enough to ride—everybody else got off.
- Multiply by 2 because the ride cost $2.00.
- Subtract 5037 pieces of popcorn that flew up in the air.
- Add 600 because 600 other people watched the popcorn fall!
- Turn your calculator upside down for the answer.

For an American history lesson, multiply 33928.75 by 12. Now turn your calculator upside down and read the name of a famous Civil War battleground!

You'll want to try this puzzle again and again. Pick any number; then add it to the next-highest number (8+9, 256+257, for example). Now, add 9, divide by 2, and subtract the original number. The answer will always be the same no matter what your starting number is.

Punch the following numbers on your calculator. Turn your calculator upside down and write the word you find.

7718 _____	7334 _____
7714 _____	818 _____
7738 _____	77345 _____
8078 _____	345 _____
40 _____	3045 _____
3704 _____	7735 _____

Answers: bill, hill, bell, blob, oh, hole, heel, bib, shell, she, shoe, sell.

Lorraine McCarty
Versailles, KY

Pattern

Enlarge and color.
Use on a New Year's
bulletin board.
See also the
pattern on page 160.

Pattern

Enlarge and color.
Use on a New Year's
bulletin board.
See also the pattern
on page 159.

It's A Deal!

I, _____, agree to write
(student name)

my daily homework assignments on this sheet. I will sign
my initials each night after I complete all assignments.
My teacher will initial my assignment card when I turn in
all my homework the next day.

♥ Monday ♥

Student _____
Teacher _____

♦ Tuesday ♦

Student _____
Teacher _____

♣ Wednesday ♣

Student _____
Teacher _____

♠ Thursday ♠

Student _____
Teacher _____

♥ Friday ♥

Student _____
Teacher _____

Teacher Note

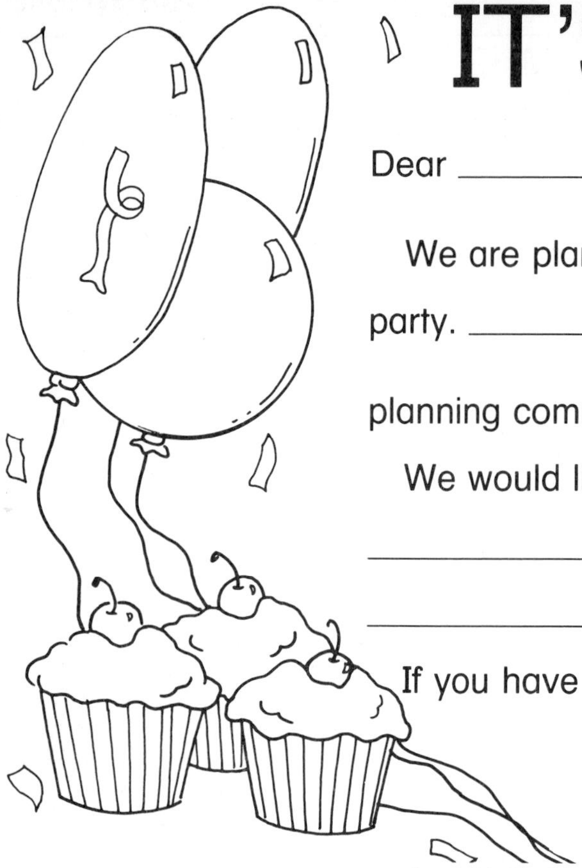

IT'S A PARTY!!!

Dear ______________________________,
(parent)

We are planning our ______________________________

party. ______________________________ is on our
(student)

planning committee.

We would like to ask you to please send ______________

______________________________ to school on

______________________________.
(date)

If you have any questions, please call me at school.

Thank you,

____
(teacher)

Teacher Note

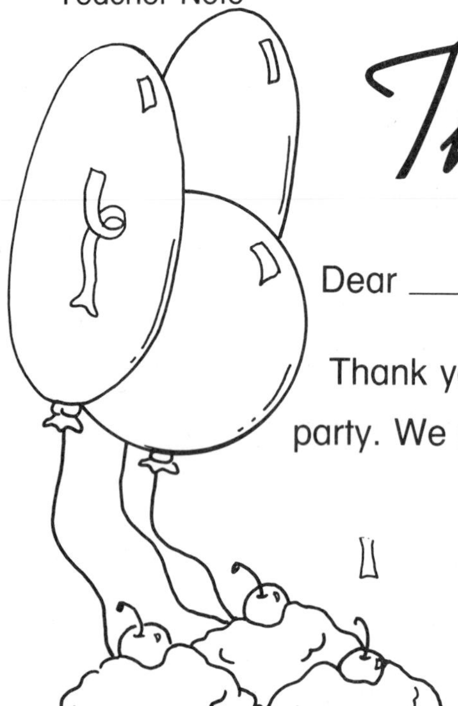

Thank you!

Dear ______________________________,
(parent)

Thank you for your help with the ______________________________

party. We really appreciated it!

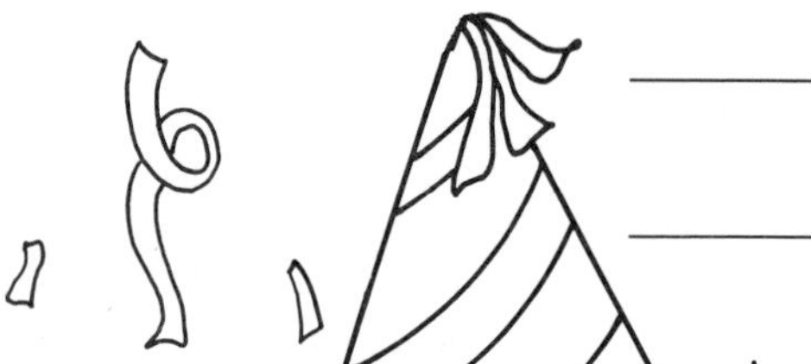

______________________________'s
(teacher)

______________________ Grade Class
(grade)

Note to teacher: Form a student committee for each class party. The committee decides (with teacher guidance) the food it would like served. The committee completes and takes home copies of the top form requesting treats or other items. The bottom form is completed and sent to parents who contributed to the party.—Idea by Jan Drehmel—Gr. 4, Chippewa Falls, WI

SCHOOL BUS

304

Now That We're Back...

Our field trip is over. So what did you think? Fill in the blanks.

1. Write a paragraph describing our field trip.

_____

_____

_____

_____

2. What was your favorite part of the trip? _____

_____

_____

3. List at least three things you learned. _____

_____

_____

4. Would you recommend this place to your friends? _____

5. What was there about the field trip that you didn't like? _____

_____

_____

6. Evaluate your own behavior on this trip. Circle one.
   I displayed: (A) excellent behavior   (C) fair behavior
                   (B) good behavior   (D) poor behavior

   Explain your answer: _____

   _____

   _____

Packing All My Bags

A research report or project needs good plans!
Fill in each suitcase <u>before</u> you begin your report.
Write on the back of this sheet if you need more space.
Ask your teacher to check your plans before you start your report.

The topic of my report will be:

_____

_____

_____

Questions my report will answer:
1. _____
2. _____
3. _____

Sources I'll use: (check)
☐ Card catalog
☐ Librarian
☐ Encyclopedias
☐ Other books
☐ Other: _____

Sources I'll use: (fill in)

Encyclopedia (name, volume, and page): _____

_____

_____

Books (titles): _____

_____

_____

_____

Materials I'll need:

_____

_____

_____

Bonus Box: Make a folder from construction paper. Staple this sheet inside. Use the folder to hold notes for your report. Decorate the front of the folder to illustrate your topic.

Fishy Rewards

Using the patterns, have each student make his own fishbowl by stapling clear plastic to construction paper. For each good job, a student may add a fish to his bowl. It's fun to see who can accumulate the most fish during a marking period or during the entire year.

LuAnn Kosiba
Northbridge, MA
1980

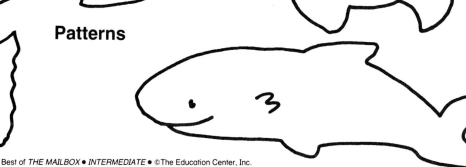

Patterns

Best of *THE MAILBOX* ● *INTERMEDIATE* ● ©The Education Center, Inc.

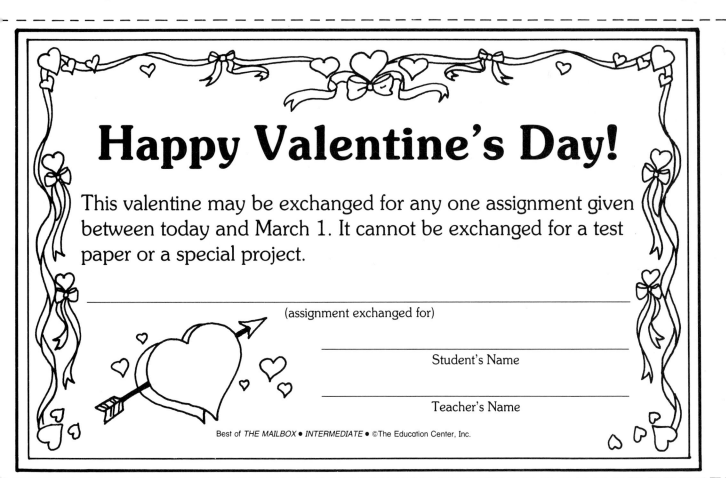

Happy Valentine's Day!

This valentine may be exchanged for any one assignment given between today and March 1. It cannot be exchanged for a test paper or a special project.

_____
(assignment exchanged for)

_____
Student's Name

_____
Teacher's Name

Best of *THE MAILBOX* ● *INTERMEDIATE* ● ©The Education Center, Inc.

Note To Teacher: Duplicate this award on colored paper for Valentine's Day. Children enjoy trading in their valentines in place of assigned work. When a child turns in his valentine, I initial it and record it in my grade book in place of the assignment grade by drawing a ♡. —Idea by Lois Cooper, Beckley, WV

Teacher's Report Card

Help your teacher by completing this form.

A. Rate your teacher on each item using a scale of 1-10 (with 10 being the highest score).

Neatness _____   Helpfulness _____

Enthusiasm _____   Discipline _____

Fairness _____   Creativity _____

Appearance of classroom _____

B. Answer each question. If you need more space, use the back of this sheet.

1. Did you think that your teacher was too hard, too easy, or just right?
_____

2. What grade (on a scale of 1-10) would you give yourself for discipline? _____
Why? _____
_____

3. What did you like best about the school year? _____
_____
_____
_____

4. What did you like least about the school year? _____
_____
_____
_____

5. If you could change one thing about your class, what would you change? _____
_____
_____
_____

6. What did you like best about your teacher? _____
_____
_____

What did you like least? _____
_____
_____

7. If you could change one thing about your school, what would you change? _____
_____
_____

8. Do you think this was a successful year for you? _____ Why?
_____
_____

Best of THE MAILBOX • INTERMEDIATE • ©The Education Center, Inc. • Carolyn Hart, Scott Depot, WV

Note to teacher: You may wish to review the meanings of items in Part A with students before having them complete the sheet.

Puttin' On The Polish

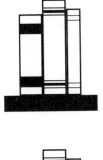

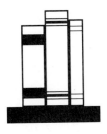

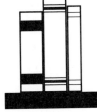

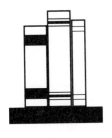

Note to teacher: Use this sheet for the first class newsletter of the year or to list supplies students will need, homework assignments, or creative writing topics.

Reproducible ©The Education Center, Inc. • THE MAILBOX

167

The Ghoulish Gourmet

Help the wicked witch increase her recipe for Coffin Cake. Multiply and fill in the chart.

Item	X2	X3	X4	X5	X6	X7	X8	X9	X10
18 snake eggs									
14 bat eyes									
27 tsp. cat's milk									
39 shark teeth									
16 ground spiders									
23 ghost hairs									
40 octopus ears									
35 toad toenails									
15 cups green slime									
51 dragon scales									

Best of *THE MAILBOX* • *INTERMEDIATE* • ©The Education Center, Inc. • Donna Frazier, Woodville, AL   Keys pp. 189-191

Eerily Yours

The following letter is missing capital letters, periods, commas, and an apostrophe.

A. Circle the letters that should be capitalized.
Add periods, commas, and an apostrophe where they are needed.

13 spooky lane
butcher hollow kentucky 43308
october 24 1987

dear count dracula

halloween is lurking just around the corner this haunted holiday would not be complete without the annual party held at the home of mr and mrs b brave

festivities will include bobbing for bats musical brooms and pin the tail on the goblin you will also have a chance to visit your fiendish friends r u squeamish frank n stein and c a ghost

the fun begins at the stroke of midnight on saturday october 31 were just dying to see you there

eerily yours
b brave

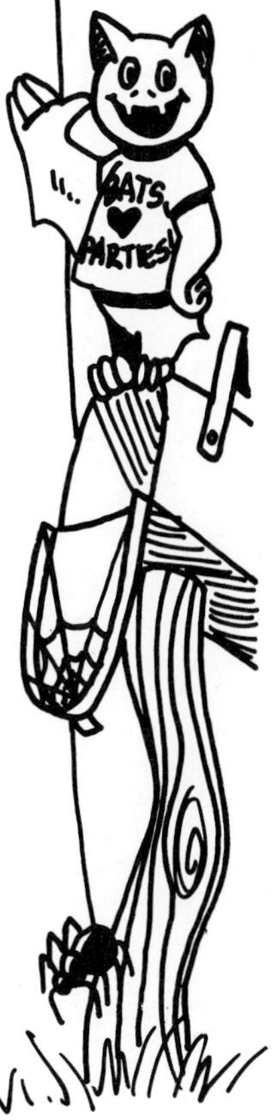

B. Pretend you are Count Dracula.
Write a response to Mr. Brave's letter on the back of this paper.

Bonus Box: Use your imagination! Draw a picture of the inside of Mr. Brave's home as he might decorate it for his party. Include pictures of his refreshments and game prizes.

Mad Libs

A mad lib is a silly, fill-in-the-blank story. To read this funny fable, number your paper from 1 to 15. Next to each number, write a plural noun (the name of something) that contains a long ē sound. Don't peek at the story until you've made your list! Then read the story and use your words to fill in the blanks. You should have a **super** silly story!

The Sugarplum Factory

The elves were hard at work getting all the treats and goodies ready

for Christmas. Over in the cookie department, they were stirring

_____1_____, _____2_____, and _____3_____ into

the batter. Wonderful smells were rising from the cake corner where

three elves were making a delicious icing out of _____4_____,

_____5_____, _____6_____, and _____7_____.

Four tiny men were creating huge candy bars: chocolate-covered

_____8_____, _____9_____, and _____10_____. The

last group was hard at work on a surprise pie full of _____11_____,

_____12_____, and _____13_____. Santa stopped by to

check on the progress. "M-m-m, delicious!" he said, with his mouth full

of _____14_____ and _____15_____.

Note To Teacher: Any word attack category may be substituted.

Blend Mad Lib

Finish each of these blends with a plural noun (the name of something); then use your list to fill in the blanks in this silly story.

1. sn _____
2. sn _____
3. gr _____
4. gr _____
5. gr _____

6. cl _____
7. cl _____
8. sp _____
9. sp _____
10. sp _____

11. fr _____
12. fr _____
13. tr _____
14. tr _____
15. tr _____

Christmas Eve Disaster

Poor Santa! This Christmas Eve nothing was going right. It all started when the elves loaded a bag of _____1_____ and _____2_____ into the sleigh by mistake. Then when Santa slid down the first chimney, he landed in a big pile of ____3____, ____4____, and ____5____. What a mess! At another house, Santa stumbled over _____6_____ and _____7_____ before he found the Christmas tree. Up in the air once more, St. Nick and his reindeer found themselves flying through clouds of _____8_____, _____9_____, and _____10_____. "This is like a bad dream," groaned Santa. Suddenly he felt something crawling on his neck. "Oh, no! _____11_____ and _____12_____!" At last he finished his rounds and turned Rudolph back toward the North Pole. When the sleigh finally came to a stop, Santa realized they had landed right on top of the workshop. The only things left were a few _____13_____, _____14_____, and _____15_____. "Thank heavens this Christmas is over!"

- -

Note To Teacher: Other blends or word attack categories may be substituted.

Christmas Song Confusion

Vocabulary, alphabetical order

Help poor, confused Rudolph! Unscramble each song title and write the answer in the blank.
Then write the songs in alphabetical order in the boxes.

1.

2.

3.

4.

5.

6.

7.

8.

9.

10.

relsvi slbel

lentis ghint

ehtiw tsircahms

gljeni lbsle

ffyors eht wnsanmo

prhuold het srdeeond

derrieen

ljloy dol ts sinaclho

tellit mrdeumr oyb

reeh eomcs tsaan

ucsal

yjo ot hte rwdlo

Best of THE MAILBOX • INTERMEDIATE • ©The Education Center, Inc. • Sue Richardson, Lynchburg, VA   Keys pp. 189–191

A Little Christmas Confusion

Synonyms, homonyms, and antonyms have caused part of this famous poem by Clement Clarke Moore to lose its rhyme! Can you rewrite it to its original form?

Directions:
1. Underline the incorrect words.
   (Hint: The number at the end of each line tells you how many words you should underline.)
2. Over each underlined word, write the correct synonym, homonym, or antonym.
3. The first one is done for you.

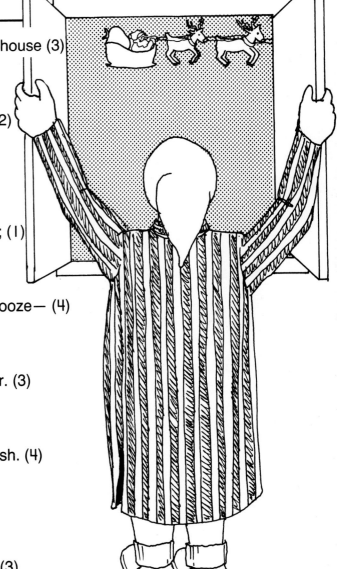

'Twas the <u>knight</u> after Christmas, when all threw the house (3)
(night written above knight)

Not a creature was mixing, knot odd a mouse; (3)

The socks were dangled by the chimney with care, (2)

Inn hopes that St. Nicholas later wood bee their; (5)

The adults were nestled all snug in they're beds; (2)

While visions of sugar-plums danced in there heads; (1)

And mamma in his 'kerchief, and eye in my cap, (2)

Had just settled our brains four a short summer's snooze— (4)

When in off the lawn there arose such a silence, (3)

I bounced from my bed two sea what was the matter. (3)

Away to the window I flu like a flash, (1)

Ripped close the shutters, and through down the sash. (4)

The sun, on the breast of the old-fallen snow, (2)

Gave the luster of midday to objects above; (1)

When, what too my wondering ayes should vanish, (3)

but a huge slay and ate itsy-bitsy reindeer, (4)

With a little elderly driver, so lively and slow, (2)

I new in a moment it must bee St. Nick. (2)

Black History Quiz

Who performed the first successful heart operation?

Decide whether each statement is true or false.
Write the correct code letter in each numbered blank.

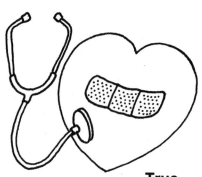

		True	False
1.	Harry Belafonte is a famous U.S. senator.	P	L
2.	Mary McLeod Bethune worked in the field of education.	N	I
3.	Andrew Young is the mayor of Chicago.	D	I
4.	The NAACP was founded by Martin Luther King.	E	W
5.	Slaves during the Civil War were not allowed to learn to read and write.	H	T
6.	Harlem is located in New York City.	S	F
7.	An abolitionist wanted slavery to end.	D	A
8.	The first black U.S. Supreme Court justice was Thurgood Marshall.	E	S
9.	Blacks and whites attended the same schools in the early part of this century.	O	M
10.	Blacks did not fight in the Civil War.	B	E
11.	Arthur Ashe is a famous baseball player.	N	L
12.	Blacks were given the right to vote in 1950.	U	A
13.	The Emancipation Proclamation freed all slaves.	A	C
14.	Jackie Robinson was the first black professional baseball player.	A	R
15.	Benjamin Banneker established the first blood bank.	G	L
16.	The first slaves were brought to America as indentured servants.	L	W
17.	Matthew Henson and Estevanico were both black explorers.	I	O
18.	The Civil War began in 1861.	I	V

__ __ __ __ __ __   __ __ __ __   __ __ __ __ __ __ __ __
7 12 2 17 10 15   5 13 1 8   4 18 11 16 3 14 9 6

Best of THE MAILBOX • INTERMEDIATE • ©The Education Center, Inc. • Becky Simpson, Winston-Salem, NC   Keys pp. 189-191

For The Incurable Romantic

Read each statement. Decide on the part of speech of the underlined word. Circle the letter in the appropriate column. Fill the circled letters in the numbered blanks below to find out the mouse's message.

What did the mouse say to his valentine?

	Noun	Verb	Adjective	Adverb
1. Dad can be a real <u>sweetheart</u>.	L	B	T	R
2. Their <u>beloved</u> neighbor moved away.	O	U	I	A
3. Some cards and letters are <u>sentimental</u>.	M	C	N	S
4. The invitation was <u>lovingly</u> shared with families far and wide.	V	D	L	H
5. His <u>thoughtful</u> nature comes through in little ways.	U	A	E	I
6. <u>Romance</u> has prompted many couples to be married on Valentine's Day.	T	B	G	W
7. People have <u>cherished</u> special memories from reunions for many years.	Y	E	A	O
8. The young mother <u>fondly</u> patted the baby's blanket.	O	W	I	E
9. Each <u>endearment</u> whispered by the princess went unnoticed until she met Prince Charming.	H	L	K	T
10. It's all right for sons to give <u>affectionate</u> hugs to their parents.	W	Z	V	G
11. A single rose can send the <u>dearest</u> message.	A	U	E	Y
12. Harps played <u>romantically</u> as the people danced.	Q	X	P	Z
13. With <u>love</u> and understanding, Martin Luther King, Jr., hoped to unite humankind.	A	Y	C	U
14. Our pet is a <u>darling</u> mouse.	Y	O	I	E
15. Families need to make time to share <u>precious</u> moments.	D	R	B	T
16. The common people have <u>adored</u> the Queen Mother in Great Britain over the years.	P	C	K	S
17. Dogs of many breeds make <u>loving</u> pets for children.	R	J	N	F
18. Birds sang <u>sweetly</u> after the thunderstorm soaked the fields.	A	I	U	E
19. The campers' <u>affection</u> for their counselor grew during their week of canoeing.	W	C	T	S
20. The youngster's <u>adoring</u> eyes pleased his teacher.	F	Y	S	X

What did the mouse say to his valentine?

__ __ __ __ __ E __ __ __ __ ! __ __ M Y
16 4 11 7 20   19 9 2 12   15 5

__ __ __ __ __ __ __ __ __ , P L E A S E.
10 13 1 18 17 6 14 3 8

Keys pp. 189-191

A Springtime Celebration

Mardi Gras is a colorful and festive celebration held on Shrove Tuesday, the day before Lent begins. The date of Mardi Gras depends on the date of Easter. Mardi Gras means *Fat Tuesday* in French. The celebration takes place at the end of a carnival season which begins on January 6. Mardi Gras is observed in many countries and states. The most famous celebration is held in New Orleans, Louisiana. Organizations called *krewes* sponsor parties, parades, and other activities during the carnival season. On Mardi Gras Day, krewe members dress in fancy costumes and masks. They take part in a large parade of beautiful floats and marching bands.

Directions: Circle each Mardi Gras word below in the puzzle.
Words can be found horizontally, vertically, or diagonally.

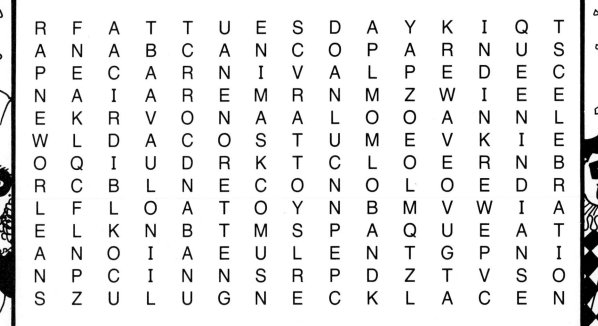

```
R F A T T U E S D A Y K I Q T
A N A B C A N C O P A R N U S
P E C A R N I V A L P E D E C
N A I A R E M R N M Z W I E E
E K R V O N A A L O O A N N L
W L D A C O S T U M E V K I E
O Q I U D R K T C L O E R N B
R C B L N E C O N O L O E D R
L F L O A T O Y N B M V W I A
E L K N B T M S P A Q U E A T
A N O I A E U L E N T G P N I
N P C I N N S R P D Z T V S O
S Z U L U G N E C K L A C E N
```

Fat Tuesday   king   Indians
mask   queen   Zulu
costume   Lent   krewe
band   carnival   necklace
float   Comus   toys
celebration   parade   New Orleans

Bonus Box: On the final day before Mardi Gras, King Zulu the ruler leads a parade in New Orleans. Find the meaning of Comus in an encyclopedia. Write it on the back of this sheet.

Best of *THE MAILBOX* ● *INTERMEDIATE* ● ©The Education Center, Inc. ● Gilda Porter, Cleveland, OH   Keys pp. 189–191

Spotlight On Shamrocks

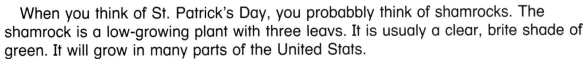

Read the story and circle 20 misspelled words.
Write the misspelled words correctly below.
Use a dictionary to help you.

When you think of St. Patrick's Day, you probabbly think of shamrocks. The shamrock is a low-growing plant with three leavs. It is usualy a clear, brite shade of green. It will grow in many parts of the United Stats.

The name *shamrock* comes from *seamrog*, witch means *three-leaved*. An Irish legund about the shamrock says it was planted in Ireland by St. Patrick when he was a missionery. He used it in his teachings to explane Christianity. It has been a symble of Ireland for hunderds of years.

The shamrock, thisel, and rose are on the Britush coat of arms becuse they are the nationel flowers of Ireland, Scotland, and Ingland.

Many folks thrughout the world wear shamrocks on St. Patrick's Day, which is selebrated on March 17. How many poeple wearing shamrocks will you nottice on St. Patrick's Day?

1. _____
2. _____
3. _____
4. _____
5. _____
6. _____
7. _____
8. _____
9. _____
10. _____

11. _____
12. _____
13. _____
14. _____
15. _____
16. _____
17. _____
18. _____
19. _____
20. _____

Ten of the words in the story are proper nouns. List these words correctly below. (Hint: Two of the proper nouns are used as adjectives in the story.) Write each word only once.

1. St. Patrick's Day
2. _____
3. _____

4. _____
5. _____
6. _____

7. _____
8. _____
9. _____
10. _____

Bonus Box: Finish this story on another sheet of paper. "Was I surprised when I opened up the cereal box and out popped an angry leprechaun, covered in corn flakes!" Add a picture to the story when you're finished.

White House Easter Eggs

Solve these problems.

1. The White House lawn is the scene of the annual Easter Egg Roll. If volunteers have collected 7,200 plastic eggs, 4,800 real eggs, and 3,000 wooden eggs for the occasion, how many eggs will be on the lawn?

2. Many of the wooden eggs are signed by famous athletes, authors, artists, and congresspersons. If 1,276 wooden eggs are signed, how many are unsigned?

3. Only children under age eight and their parents can participate. If 10,288 of the 29,104 participants are parents, how many are children?

4. The Egg Roll starts at 10 a.m. and ends at 2 p.m. How many hours does the event last?

5. Fifty children at a time search for eggs in different areas of the lawn. How many groups of children look for eggs if 10,550 children are divided into groups?

6. The children race by rolling eggs with plastic scoops down eight lanes. There is one child in each lane. If it takes five minutes for each race, how long will it take for 80 children to roll eggs?

7. Each lane is 24 feet long. How many feet of ribbon are needed to rope off eight lanes side by side?

8. The Navy, Army, Air Force, and Marine bands play music on the lawn. If there are 75 members in each band, how many musicians will play?

9. The first Easter Egg Roll on the White House lawn was 111 years ago when Rutherford B. Hayes was president. In what year was the first White House Egg Roll?

10. Decorated Easter eggs are on display at the White House. There are 180 eggs on display. How many dozen eggs are on display?

Hop, Hop, Hooray!

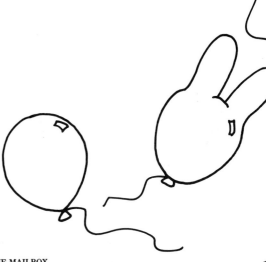

What In The World?

What might you do with each of the following things?
Look up each word in the dictionary and write it under the correct heading.

endive	wallaby	mousse	fez	ketch
sari	bateau	dugong	hansom	soufflé
sloop	toga	puffin	umiak	ascot
cuscus	stoat	fennel	piccalilli	serape

EAT IT . . .

WEAR IT . . .

CAGE IT . . .

RIDE IN IT . . .

 Best of *THE MAILBOX* • *INTERMEDIATE* • ©The Education Center, Inc. • Pamela Klawitter, Mt. Nebo, WV   Keys pp. 189-191

Now You're Cooking!

1.
List 10 ways to mash a potato. Be creative!

2.
Write a recipe for happiness. Include ingredients and steps.

3.
How many states can you name? List them. Check your spelling with a dictionary.

4.
Draw a picture of "The Perfect Classroom." List 10 words to describe it.

5.
Do you wear a manse or do you live in it? Do you eat a salmagundi or wear it? Use a dictionary to find out.

6.
How many national parks are in the U.S.? Use an encyclopedia to find out. Which park is nearest to your home?

7.
Plan the perfect Halloween Party. Describe your costume, refreshments, games. List five famous people you would invite.

8.
List a noun for every letter in the alphabet. Use a dictionary to help you. Try verbs next!

9.
Design a greeting card to give a student who is new to your school.

10.
"A duck is a quacker. A cookie is a snacker." Create 10 other two-line rhymes.

11.
Make up 10 math problems with answers that equal 20. Examples: $11+3+6=20$; $999-979=20$.

12.
Draw a picture to illustrate each feeling:
Worry
Joy
Excitement
Anger

13.
List 10 things you would like to accomplish before you are 20 years old.

14.
Design a healthy menu for a new restaurant. Include the price and food group of each item.

15.
Write a letter to your favorite rock group or star. Describe yourself and tell why you like music.

Directions: Here are 15 fun things to do when you finish your work.

Color each steam cloud as you complete the activity.

Note to teacher: See instructions for using this sheet on page 98.

Can You Believe It?

Copy each fact on your paper in your best cursive writing. Skip 1-2 lines after each fact. Now, cut out and glue a circle at the end of each fact on your paper.

1. The first gambling dice were actually the ankle bones of sheep.

2. The kangaroo rat will die unless it takes frequent dust baths.

3. Empress Elizabeth of Russia owned 15,000 dresses —all pink.

4. Cowboy actor Freeman Clark trained his horse to roller skate.

5. A water beetle can kill a frog 20 times its own size.

6. A sulphur-crested cockatoo, owned by an Australian woman, lived to the age of 120.

7. The common shrew eats its own weight in food.

8. An elephant in the Franconi Circus expertly played the harmonica in 1820.

For these and more strange facts, refer to Ripley's <u>Believe It or Not!</u> published by Pocket Books.

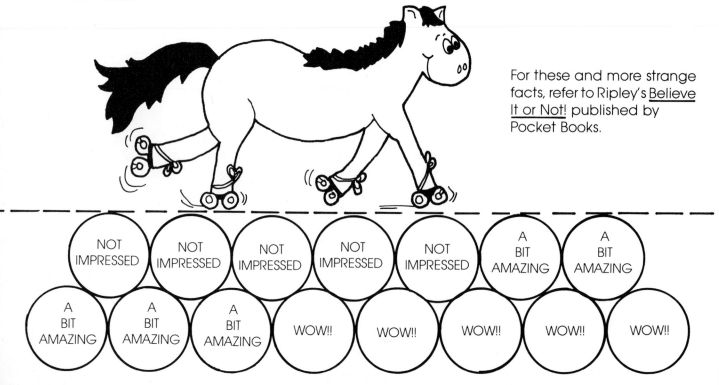

Rebecca G. Simpson
Winston-Salem, NC

Zero Multiplication

Across

A. 404 × 4
C. 500 × 8
D. 707 × 7
F. 700 × 7

G. 505 × 5
K. 901 × 3
M. 50 × 5
P. 49 × 4

R. 606 × 6
S. 70 × 7
U. 609 × 6

Down

A. 400 × 3
B. 300 × 6
C. 202 × 2
E. 303 × 3
G. 300 × 9

H. 400 × 5
J. 105 × 7
L. 500 × 9
N. 105 × 3
Q. 808 × 8

T. 305 × 3
U. 10 × 3
V. 60 × 6

Famous Women Word Find

Find these 22 famous women's names horizontally, vertically and diagonally in the puzzle. Look forward and backward. Then choose five names to find in encyclopedias or reference books. Briefly write why each woman is famous.

```
A N N I E O W O L N O D R O G E T T E I L U J
M C L A R A G B N B A R G Y N O T I V J U E O J
A L P E A S L O N E R B S I T R H C C U S R C E
R I M A R H A K L U N A S I C L H L E R C A R L
M L T O N I C S B D A L B C L M P A J I T A M L
A L M A T R G R U M A M I D K J A R E A A M E Y
R I V S E L J K L N O M E E F G K A S W M C T O
G A J A N E A D D A M S E H B I L B C A N M E F
A N V N C Y U Z Z Y A I S I T L E A I R Y L I E
R H I N H C F E I S R T R T R H Y R S D N R A H
E E P I E H T O O T I T Y P R O H T A H R A E I
T L E E I I L S C H A R Y I N G S O R O A E H C
T L A O R S S U S A N B A T N E L A E H A R H L
H M R A U H K O E R A T N U N I R E I C H E R H
A A L K C O A Y L O N S U N I R E I C H E H A T
T N S L E L T R E L D E O K L T B L G A L A R A
C A B E I M B E E B E L L E B O Y D L E C R T I
H C U Y R R O R E K R A P Y H T O R O D L E C R
E H C E A A C A I H S S A N E D N A R O R K S B
R A K L M J E S S J O A N E B A E Z O E G S O I
I C A G E R A L D I N E F E R R A R O N O I R A
M A R R U M A R Y M C L E O D B E T H U N E C M
L A U R A I N G A L L S W I L D E R T N Y C N
```

Maria Tallchief
Dorothy Parker
Laura Ingalls Wilder
Annie Oakley
Joan Baez
Lillian Hellman
Belle Boyd
Juliette Gordon Low

Margaret Thatcher
Golda Meir
Julia Ward Howe
Amelia Earhart
Marie Curie
Nellie Bly
Pearl S. Buck
Geraldine Ferraro

Rachel Carson
Shirley Chisholm
Jane Addams
Clara Barton
Marian Anderson
Susan B. Anthony
Mary McLeod Bethune

Math Trailblazer

Directions: Begin with this number: _____. Move along the trail by following directions according to the shape in the code. Write your answer in each figure on the trail. Show your work on another sheet of paper.

CODE:

△ Add 2,459   ◯ Subtract 1,423   ▢ Subtract 109

START

STOP

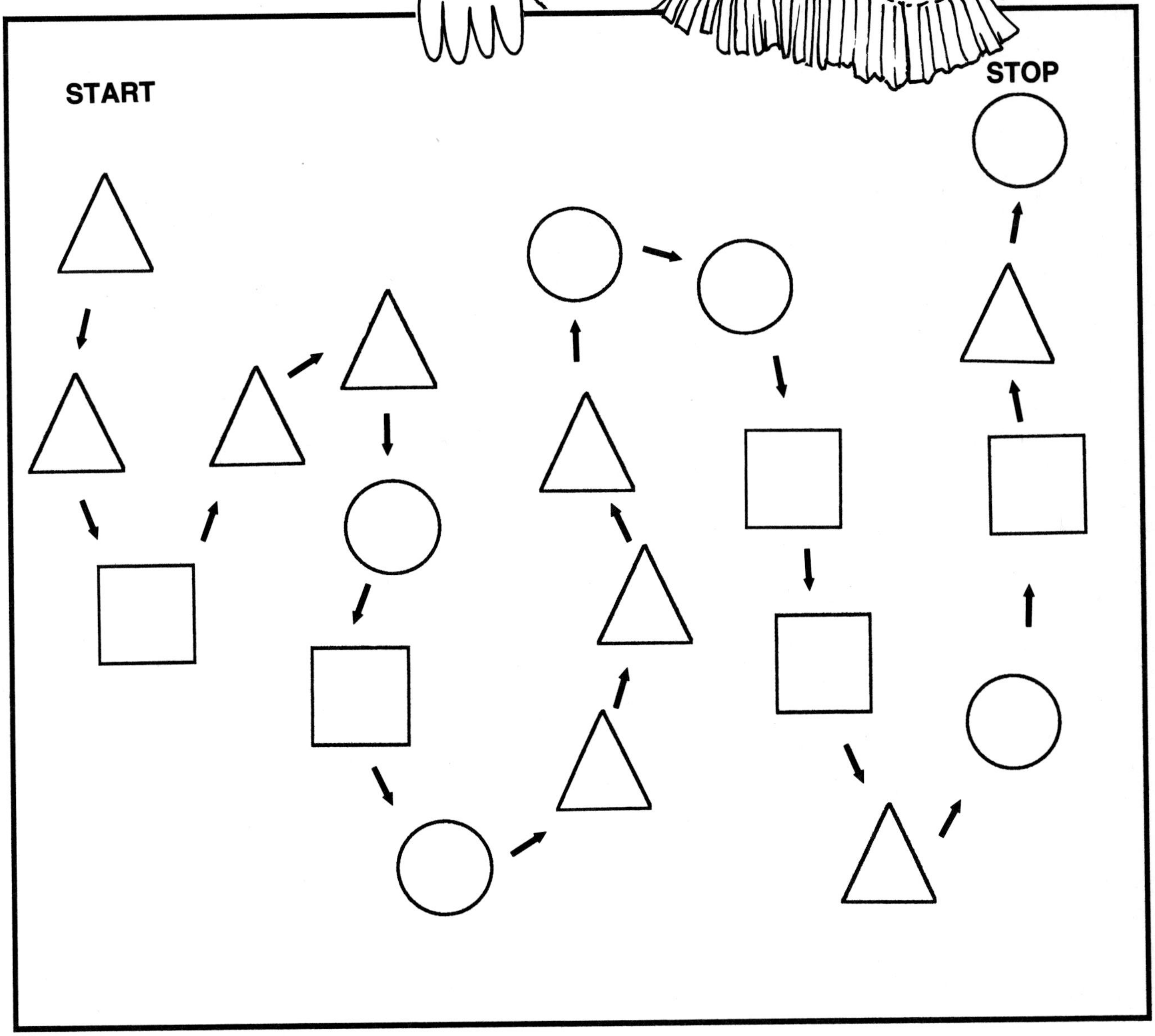

Best of THE MAILBOX ● INTERMEDIATE ● ©The Education Center, Inc. ● Jeanne Mullineaux, Unadilla, NY

Note To Teacher: Fill in the blank in the directions with a number before duplication. To adapt, white-out the directions/numbers in the code and add new ones.

Make Up Your Mind

Underline the solution you would choose for each problem below.
If you have a better solution than the choices given, write it in the "other" blank.

1.

You have caught 6 fish on the first day at a quiet lake. On the second day, you have already caught 9 fish in the first hour, all bigger than yesterday's fishes. The law allows you to catch 15 fish. What do you do?
a. Go home with the 15 fish you've already caught
b. Continue to fish and keep everything you catch
c. Continue to fish and keep only the 15 biggest fish
d. Other _____

2.

You have found a young opossum which you have raised to maturity. Your landlord has just told you that you can't keep the animal in your apartment any longer. What do you do?
a. Call the local wildlife center to ask for advice
b. Take the opossum to a local zoo
c. Release it back in the forest
d. Keep it as a pet anyway
e. Other _____

3.

While you are deer hunting with a friend, he shoots a small falcon. As you are leaving the woods, a game warden walks up to both of you. He asks if you know anything about a falcon that was illegally shot. What do you do?
a. Tell the game warden that your friend shot the falcon
b. Say that you don't know anything about the shooting
c. Say nothing but call the game warden later to tell him about your friend
d. Other _____

4.

A man has been charged with shooting a deer out of season. The man does not have a job. He says he shot the deer to provide meat for his hungry family. You are on the jury which must decide on his case. What do you do?
a. Make him pay a fine of $400
b. Set him free with a warning
c. Send him to jail for six months
d. Other _____

Now, on the back of this sheet give the reasons for your choices.

Write a paragraph for each choice.

Bonus Box: Choose one of these animals. Draw a picture of it in its natural habitat.

Who was the first president to have his inaugural address broadcast over the radio?

Supply the ending punctuation for each sentence. Then circle the letter under the correct sentence type. Put the letter in the blank with the same number as the sentence.

	Exclamatory	Declarative	Imperative	Interrogative
1. Please close the door	G	T	N	L
2. Did Susie leave for school yet	A	E	U	O
3. Yes, she and Eliza left earlier than usual	N	C	M	Q
4. How big the monster's teeth are	E	I	A	U
5. Anne-Louise and Tara took the books to the library	T	L	V	W
6. Have Remy and Ashok finished their math	L	M	P	C
7. What an amazingly long snake that is	V	H	C	F
8. Give Elliott and Jan your papers when you finish	E	Y	A	W
9. Please take Erin to the clinic	X	T	L	R
10. This afternoon Tres, Jarrett, and Marshall will play the recorder	P	G	J	H
11. What a big sandwich you have	I	O	E	A
12. Did Anne Elise return the umbrella yet	B	D	F	O
13. Seven silly snails crawled along the sidewalk	R	D	K	H
14. Have Andy and Jim arrived at the party	P	K	Q	I

‾3‾ ‾8‾ ‾5‾ ‾7‾ ‾11‾ ‾1‾   ‾6‾ ‾12‾ ‾2‾ ‾9‾ ‾14‾ ‾13‾ ‾10‾ ‾4‾

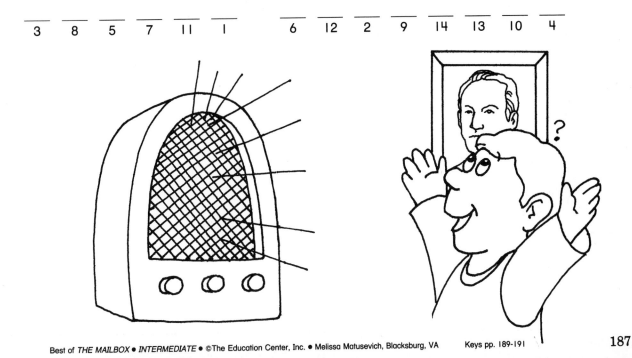

And Now For The News

Current events

Use today's newspaper to fill in the chart below.
Use the following scale to fill in the last column:

Very important—★ ★ ★ ★
Important—★ ★ ★
Not very important—★ ★
Not at all important—★

	NAME	JOB OR POSITION	WHY PERSON IS IN THE NEWS	RANK FOR THIS NEWS ITEM
U.S. government official				
World leader (other than the United States)				
Local personality (government or other than government)				
Famous sports, television, or movie personality				

Now pick one of the persons you recorded. Write your own news story about that person on the back of this sheet.

Best of THE MAILBOX • INTERMEDIATE • ©The Education Center, Inc. • Rebecca Simpson, Winston-Salem, NC

Answer Key

Page 80

	NOUN	VERB	ADVERB	ADJECTIVE
1. The female rabbit is called the doe, and the male is called the buck.	(O)	J	C	E
2. A nest of dry grass is lined with down from the doe's body.	L	O	M	(R)
3. A newborn rabbit is hairless and blind.	I	B	K	(A)
4. Rabbits signal to each other by displaying their white tails.	T	(F)	N	T
5. They prefer to go out at night and sleep during the day.	J	(P)	S	A
6. Rabbits defend themselves by keeping still or by running away.	C	G	(W)	E
7. They can run up to forty miles an hour.	I	L	H	(O)
8. They change directions quickly to confuse the enemy.	N	Q	(E)	F
9. In autumn, rabbits eat more to prepare for winter's slim food supply.	(R)	K	P	M
10. The rabbit's senses of smell and hearing are very sharp.	D	J	(T)	O

A rabbit's fur is tightly packed, which helps make it

W A T E R P R O O F
6 3 10 8 2 5 9 1 7 4

Cottontails
desert cottontail
eastern cottontail
mountain cottontail
New England cottontail

Domestic Rabbits
Angora
Belgian hare
Californian
Chinchilla
Florida White
Havana
Netherland Dwarf
New Zealand
Palomino
Rex
White Flemish Giant

Page 175

Noun	Verb	Adjective	Adverb
(L)	B	T	R
(O)	U	(I)	A
M	C	(N)	S
V	D	L	(H)
U	A	(E)	I
(T)	B	G	W
Y	(E)	A	O
O	W	I	(E)
(H)	L	K	T
W	Z	(V)	G
A	U	(E)	Y
Q	X	P	(Z)
(A)	Y	C	U
Y	O	(I)	E
D	R	(B)	T
P	(C)	K	S
R	J	(N)	F
A	I	U	(E)
(W)	C	T	S
F	Y	(S)	X

Answer to riddle: Cheese Whiz! Be My Valentine, Please.

Page 174

True	False
P	(L)
(N)	I
D	(I)
E	(W)
(H)	T
	F
(S)	A
(D)	S
(E)	(M)
O	
	(E)
B	(L)
N	(A)
U	C
(A)	R
(A)	(L)
G	W
(L)	O
(I)	V
(I)	

Answer to riddle: Daniel Hale Williams

Page 90

Finish each sentence by writing the correct number on the dolphin.

Karana lived alone on the island . . . 9

Karana's father was . . . 3

Karana's best friend on the island was . . . 5

Karana was left behind because . . . 1

A girl who came with the Aleut hunters . . . 15

Tainor and Lurai were . . . 11

Karana's fence around her house was . . . 14

Karana's brother, Ramo, was . . . 7

Karana tried to leave the island by . . . 13

When Karana finally left on the white men's ship, she . . . 6

Ulape was . . . 8

Karana liked her cormorant skirt better than . . . 10

Page 94
(Answers may vary.)

I. Body of a beaver
   A. Known for wide, flat tail
   B. Uses tail to steer when swimming
   C. Strong front teeth for cutting trees
II. Where beavers live
   A. In dams and lodges in rivers and streams
   B. Live in groups called colonies
III. Diet of beavers
   A. Bark
   B. Twigs
   C. Leaves
   D. Roots
IV. Young beavers
   A. Called kits or pups
   B. Stay with adults for two years
   C. Sent away from family

Page 137
1. The matador and his assistants enter the ring.
2. The bull enters the ring.
3. The matador gracefully moves his cape.
4. The picador enters the ring.
5. The picador pokes the bull with a pole.
6. A bugle is blown.
7. The banderillero pushes three sticks into the bull.
8. The matador moves with a hidden sword.
9. The matador kills the bull.

Page 178
1. 15,000 eggs
2. 1,724 unsigned eggs
3. 18,816 children
4. 4 hours
5. 211 groups
6. 50 minutes
7. 216 feet
8. 300 musicians
9. 1877
10. 15 dozen

Page 107
1. $44.00
2. 12 bandages
3. 175 pounds
4. 41 towels
5. 25 trunks
6. 27 feet
7. $52.33
8. $3,000.00
9. 224 pounds
10. $78.70
11. $706.50
12. $135.00

Page 112

1. Ann, did you help plan the annual picnic?
2. Tom Sales, our fire chief, said that the cause of the fire might be arson.
3. Yes, I saw a famous entertainer when I visited Hollywood, California.
4. How long does it take to drive from Mobile, Alabama to St. Louis, Missouri?
5. The sound of the echo goes bouncing from the hillside, to the canyon, and to the valley below.
6. The students wanted to go to Del Rio, Texas or Acapulco, Mexico.
7. The music attracted large crowds to the concert in Chicago, Illinois.

14 Cove Creek
Latara, Tennessee
August 16, 1987

Dear Aunt Hattie,

Thanks for such a practical, fun gift. Boards, nails, hinges, a hammer, and plans for a birdhouse—what more could anyone ask for?

Your niece,
Toni

Page 113

●	Ⓑ	1. We used a net to land the huge, flopping fish.
●	Ⓒ	2. After the storm had passed, workers cleared the roads.
Ⓓ	●	3. Many friends gathered at Tom's house; it was a party.
●	Ⓗ	4. The program, which started at 7:00, lasted two hours.
Ⓘ	●	5. Jack knows how to handle applause; he is often in the winner's circle.
●	Ⓣ	6. Maureen, I think, decided to go to Six Flags.
●	Ⓙ	7. A squatty frog, which eats tons of insects, has lived under our porch for years.
●	Ⓛ	8. Before you leave school, make sure you're ready for the play.
Ⓑ	●	9. Mother likes to go to the mountains; Dad prefers the beach.
●	Ⓜ	10. Piles of lovely, colorful gifts were on the table.

Unscramble the letters in the comma column to find the name of the most mysterious shoe: S N E A K E R

Page 136

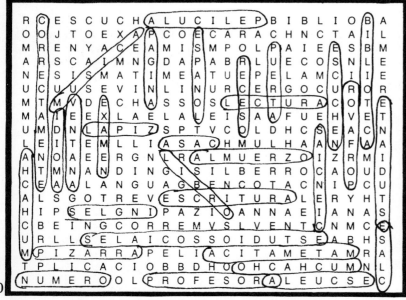

Page 172

1. Frosty The Snowman
2. Here Comes Santa Claus
3. Jingle Bells
4. Jolly Old St. Nicholas
5. Joy To The World
6. Little Drummer Boy
7. Rudolph, The Red-Nosed Reindeer
8. Silent Night
9. Silver Bells
10. White Christmas

Page 177

1.	probably	11.	hundreds
2.	leaves	12.	thistle
3.	usually	13.	British
4.	bright	14.	because
5.	States	15.	national
6.	which	16.	England
7.	legend	17.	throughout
8.	missionary	18.	celebrated
9.	explain	19.	people
10.	symbol	20.	notice

1.	St. Patrick's Day	6.	Christianity
2.	United States	7.	British
3.	Irish	8.	Scotland
4.	Ireland	9.	England
5.	St. Patrick	10.	March

Page 180

Eat It	Wear It
endive	sari
mousse	toga
fennel	fez
soufflé	ascot
piccalilli	serape
Cage It	**Ride In It**
cuscus	sloop
wallaby	bateau
stoat	hansom
dugong	umiak
puffin	ketch

Page 142

1. Bismarck
2. Springfield
3. Olympia
4. Olympia, Tallahassee, Richmond, Augusta
5. Santa Fe
6. Richmond
7. Springfield, Lansing
8. Olympia
9. Austin

1. blizzard
2. lunar
3. earthquake
4. amount
5. atmosphere
6. lightning
7. up
8. ray
9. melts
10. news
Answer to riddle: an umbrella

Answer Key

Page 183

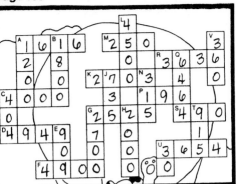

Page 169

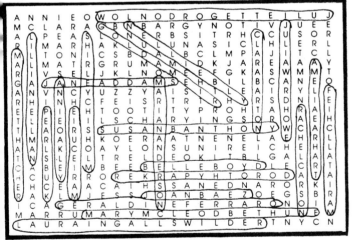

Page 184

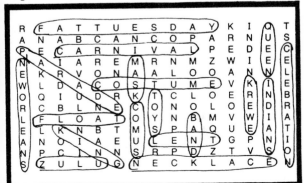

Page 176

R	F	A	T	T	U	E	S	D	A	Y	K	I		T
A	N	A	B	C	A	N	C	O	P	A	R	E		S
P	E	I	C	A	R	N	I	V	A	L	E	U		C
N	W	I	A	R	E	M	M	R	N	M	W	E		E
E	K	D	N	V	O	N	A	A	L	Z	A	N		L
W	L	O	I	A	D	K	R	L	O	O	V	I		E
O	Q	B	V	D	R	E	D	O	L	U	E	N		B
R	C	L	A	N	E	B	I	R	E	W	R	D		R
L	F	L	O	A	T	K	G	Q	U	E	K	I		A
E	L	N	C	M	B	O	R	M	N	B	R	A		T
A	N	I	K	U	S	R	A	B	M	U	E	N		I
N	P	C	I	S	N	N	S	P	D	Z	W	S		O
S	Z	U	L	U	G	N	E	C	K	L	A	C	E	N

Answer to Bonus Box: Comus, founded in 1857, is the oldest krewe.

Page 187

Exclamatory	Declarative	Imperative	Interrogative
G	T	(N)	L
A	E	C	Q
N	I	U	U
(E)	I	M	W
T	L	A	(C)
L	M	V	F
(V)	H	P	W
E	Y	C	R
X	T	(A)	H
P	(G)	(L)	H
		J	
I	O	E	A
B	D	F	(O)
R	(D)	K	(H)
P	K	Q	(I)

Answer to riddle: Calvin Coolidge

Page 168

X2	X3	X4	X5	X6	X7	X8	X9	X 10
36	54	72	90	108	126	144	162	180
28	42	56	70	84	98	112	126	140
54	81	108	135	162	189	216	243	270
78	117	156	195	234	273	312	351	390
32	48	64	80	96	112	128	144	160
46	69	92	115	138	161	184	207	230
80	120	160	200	240	280	320	360	400
70	105	140	175	210	245	280	315	350
30	45	60	75	90	105	120	135	150
102	153	204	255	306	357	408	459	510

Page 83

1. Mrs. Whatsit is a friend influencing Charles Wallace.
2. Meg, the oldest sister, measures up as a math whiz.
3. Meg and Charles Wallace meet Calvin one summer day in the woods.
4. In an old house, Mrs. Who quotes famous sayings and sews speedily.
5. All five characters traveled by tesseract through the universe.
6. As Mrs. Who materializes, her tremendous spectacles twinkle.
7. The Happy Medium laughs as she stares into her crystal ball.
8. On Camazotz, Mr. Murry is being held prisoner by IT, a wicked brain.
9. IT controls and dominates everyone's lives on the planet, Camazotz.
10. Aunt Beast cares for her little, confused Meg.
11. Calvin, Father, and Meg quickly tesser to escape the power of IT.
12. Alone, Meg returns to Camazotz to rescue special, little Charles Wallace.

Page 173

'Twas the night before Christmas, when all through the house
Not a creature was stirring, not even a mouse;
The stockings were hung by the chimney with care,
In hopes that St. Nicholas soon would be there;
The children were nestled all snug in their beds
While visions of sugar-plums danced in their heads;
And mamma in her 'kerchief, and I in my cap,
Had just settled our brains for a long winter's nap—
When out on the lawn there arose such a clatter,
I sprang from my bed to see what was the matter.
Away to the window I flew like a flash,
Tore open the shutters, and threw up the sash.
The moon, on the breast of the new-fallen snow,
Gave the luster of midday to objects below;
When, what to my wondering eyes should appear,
but a miniature sleigh and eight tiny reindeer,
With a little old driver, so lively and quick,
I knew in a moment it must be St. Nick.